CASE STUDIES
IN INTERNATIONAL
BUSINESS ⸻

CASE STUDIES
IN INTERNATIONAL
BUSINESS

Christine Uber Grosse
Florida International University

Robert E. Grosse
University of Miami

 PRENTICE HALL REGENTS, Englewood Cliffs, NJ 07632

Library of Congress Cataloging-in-Publication Data

Grosse, Christine Uber.
    Case studies in international business / Christine Uber Grosse.
  Robert E. Grosse.
      p.   cm.
    Includes index.
    ISBN 0-13-119314-7
    1. International business enterprises—Management—Case studies.
  I. Grosse, Robert E.   II. Title.
HD62.4.G76 1988   87-22307
658′ .049—dc19   CIP

Editorial/production supervision and
   interior design: Patricia V. Amoroso
Cover design: Wanda Lubelska Design
Cover photo: Jane Latta
Manufacturing buyer: Margaret Rizzi

Printed in the United States of America

10   9   8   7

ISBN 0-13-119314-7

PRENTICE-HALL INTERNATIONAL (UK) LIMITED, London
PRENTICE-HALL OF AUSTRALIA PTY. LIMITED, Sydney
PRENTICE-HALL CANADA INC., Toronto
PRENTICE-HALL HISPANOAMERICANA, S.A., Mexico
PRENTICE-HALL OF INDIA PRIVATE LIMITED, New Delhi
PRENTICE-HALL OF JAPAN, INC., Tokyo
SIMON & SCHUSTER ASIA PTE. LTD., Singapore
EDITORA PRENTICE-HALL DO BRASIL, LTDA., Rio de Janeiro

To Alan and Amanda

CONTENTS ====

INTRODUCTION

PURPOSE OF THE TEXT

Case Studies in International Business combines language and content instruction through the use of the case study method. It features relevant, current topics that are directly related to the students' future studies or current jobs in management, international trade, finance, and so on. The text presents actual cases about companies and managers facing real problems, and challenges students to develop their problem-solving ability as they analyze business situations and recommend appropriate courses of action. In the process, students will master the necessary business vocabulary through a wide variety of oral and written activities. The book's critical-thinking exercises encourage students to interpret key business issues through their own observations and experience, while research activities teach students to draw on resources of the local business community. The major goal of the text is to teach Business English by means of actual cases with language-focused exercises, thus bringing the realities of the business world into the classroom.

INTENDED AUDIENCE

The level of the text is high intermediate to advanced. Its intended audience is ESL/EFL students who are pursuing or planning to pursue academic studies in business, ESL/EFL students who want to go into business, and businessmen and -women who want to improve their English. With its focus on international business, the text is designed to meet the needs of students in countries around the world as well as in the United States, Canada, and Great Britain.

SELECTION OF CASES

Individual cases were selected to cover a wide spectrum of business situations and countries. Particular effort was made to offer cases in the areas of business strategy, marketing, finance, international trade, and cross-cultural management. These subjects are of great importance to businesspeople in any country. The cases present a mixture of situations facing large and small companies, from developed and less-developed countries, and in many industries. All of the cases involve either the United States as a target market or a U.S. firm as a participant in the situation. The particular business issue of concern in each case is noted in the table of contents.

All of the cases are drawn from actual business situations. "Monster Chomp Cookies" and "HongKong & Shanghai Bank" present recent decisions made by the firms named in the cases, and the authors discussed both cases in detail with managers in those firms. The other cases either use disguised company names or present generalized problems faced by many companies such as the ones mentioned.

In most cases, the student should take the position of a company decision-maker to carry out the analysis. However, in "The U.S. Auto Industry" and in "West African Electric," it is also useful to allow students to take the viewpoint of the government involved. Generally speaking, any international business activity affects the countries involved, so the view of the government would be relevant in each case. Since our goal is to get students to think as decision-makers in the cases, the normal focus should be on company decisions.

SUGGESTIONS FOR EFFECTIVE USE OF THE TEXT

Each chapter of *Case Studies in International Business* consists of (1) prereading exercises, (2) the case itself, (3) comprehension exercises, (4) vocabulary-development exercises, (5) critical-thinking questions, (6) research activities, and (7) a case-analysis section. A glossary of business terms appears at the end of the text for reference. In order to help the student and teacher use each section most effectively, the following suggestions are offered. The instructor's manual with answer key provides additional instructions and information related to the specific cases, as well as an answer key.

Prereading Exercise

The purpose of the four thought-provoking questions at the beginning of each chapter is to help the students focus on the essential issues to be presented in the case. Discussion of key issues activates the students' background knowledge about the topics treated in the case and facilitates reading comprehension.

The teacher may start the class discussion of the prereading exercise by asking for volunteers to read a question aloud. Then the teacher may encourage students to respond to the question and react to each other's responses. As the discussion progresses, the teacher may introduce new vocabulary that is necessary to the case.

The prereading questions are likely to generate other related questions and additional discussion of the topic. The teacher can take advantage of the student-directed discussion to draw further on students' experience, opinions, and background knowledge related to the topic. In this way, the students will be well prepared to begin reading the case description.

The Case

Each case focuses on an actual or simulated business situation that presents a real business problem that the students are challenged to solve in the case-analysis section. Subsequent exercises lead the student gradually to the solution of the case while building up background knowledge and structuring the decision-making process. Additionally, the case provides a meaningful context for the language, introducing valuable business terminology and concepts.

Given the level of detail presented in each case situation, the case should probably be assigned initially as homework reading. It then can be reread in class. In both situations, it is very important that the students do the prereading exercise prior to reading the case, so that their background knowledge is activated and reading comprehension is improved. Reading the case for homework, rather than in class, offers several advantages: more class time can be spent on communicative class activities and discussion, and students are free to spend as much time reading the case as they like.

Comprehension Questions

Comprehension questions give the student an opportunity to identify the main ideas, locate key facts, and discuss concepts that are introduced. These exercises are designed to develop specific reading skills such as identifying the main idea, locating key facts, and skimming and scanning the text for detailed information. In several chapters the comprehension section also includes chart- and table-interpretation exercises.

This section can be taught in a variety of ways. Using an interactive, communicative approach, the teacher may have the students work in pairs to answer the questions orally or in writing. They may alternate asking and answering the questions, responding to each other's comments and strengthening their answers. Or the teacher may assign small groups of three to five students to discuss the answers to each question. In either instance, the teacher can circulate around the room to listen to the work of the pairs or small groups.

Another option is the whole-class approach, in which the teacher (or a student) reads the question aloud and asks for volunteers to respond.

Finally, the teacher may choose to assign the comprehension exercises as written homework, to be discussed orally or handed in at the next class meeting.

Vocabulary-Development Exercises

The purpose of the vocabulary-development exercises is to build business vocabulary through a variety of approaches, including paraphrasing activities, guessing the meaning of words from context, prefix and suffix recognition, and discussion of key terms and concepts.

Many of the vocabulary exercises lend themselves to a type of practice that involves oral communication skills rather than silent reading and written completion of the assignment. The teacher therefore can plan to let the students work in pairs on these exercises. Working with partners actively involves all students in the exercise and provides the opportunity for more oral interaction than in other approaches where only one student at a time can respond.

Critical Thinking

This section of each chapter challenges the student to use higher-level cognitive skills in making inferences, drawing conclusions, and making predictions about major issues in the case. In the critical-thinking questions the student is called on to use background knowledge, personal experience, insight, and understanding of issues presented in the text.

In order for the students to fully explore their ideas, the teacher may wish to assign them to work in small groups or with partners. In this way they can share their thoughts and experience in order to find reasonable answers to the questions. The pooling of ideas and discussion of issues help the students to develop oral language proficiency and communication strategies, while at the same time they provide them with valuable experience in reasoning and supporting their views.

Research Questions

The research questions serve a multitude of purposes. For example, they teach students how to utilize community resources, teach research and interview techniques, provide an opportunity to use the language in real business settings outside of the classroom, allow development of listening and speaking skills in a meaningful context, and encourage reading of additional authentic materials related to the case study.

Through a variety of research activities, the student becomes familiar with the resources of the local business community, and has the opportunity to interact with businessmen and -women. Each assignment is task-oriented, and has specifically outlined instructions and objectives.

The teacher may choose to allow the students to work in pairs or teams on certain projects. At other times, the students may work individually to complete the tasks.

Case Analysis

The case-analysis section completes the study of each case. The format of the section varies, but it typically involves the students in small-group work. Their tasks, which are specifically identified, generally include: identification of the problem at hand, review of the case information, analysis of the situation and its implications, proposal and defense of alternative solutions, reactions to classmates' criticisms and suggestions, and choice of an appropriate course of action.

A learner-centered classroom is essential to the case-study method of analysis. The teacher intervenes as little as possible in the work of the small groups, allowing the students to take responsibility for their own learning. The teacher acts as a facilitator or guide when needed.

Students should remember that single or precise solutions to cases are rare. Often, more than one solution is appropriate. Therefore, a logical thought process, a careful situational analysis, and the ability to communicate the reasoning behind the recommendations for action are essential parts of the case analysis.

For the students, the benefits of the case analysis will lie in the opportunity for flexible and creative language use in a meaningful context, the development of critical-thinking and problem-solving skills, and the understanding of group dynamics. As participants in case analysis, students will gain practice in sizing up a situation, considering alternative ways to approach a problem, and making decisions regarding appropriate action. These skills will serve the students well in their business careers.

ACKNOWLEDGMENTS ═══════════

We would like to acknowledge John Staczek, Assistant Dean of Languages and Linguistics at Georgetown University, who first suggested to us the idea of using case studies to teach Business English. We are also grateful to Steve Vogel and Jerry Brock, who generously helped us with the revisions of specific cases. In addition, special thanks are due to the reviewers of the manuscript for their insightful comments: Dean Jensen, Pat Haggerty, Ron Bradley, Ashley Goldhor-Wilcock, and Ann Wederspahn. We would also like to thank Brenda White, Peg Drewes, and Pattie Amoroso of Prentice-Hall for their able assistance and encouragement throughout the production process. Finally, we would like to acknowledge that the Bell South case is reprinted with permission from Robert Grosse and Duane Kujawa, *International Business*, Homewood, Ill.: Richard D. Irwin Company, 1988. This book is a useful supplement to *Case Studies in International Business*.

CASE STUDIES
IN INTERNATIONAL
BUSINESS

1

THE XM COMPANY CASE (PART A)

Comparative advantage in international trade

Photo by Robert E. Grosse

PREREADING EXERCISES

Discuss the following questions before reading the case.

1. What activities constitute international trade?

2. Why do companies engage in international trade?

3. Give examples of some companies that you know which conduct international business. What do they buy from suppliers in other countries? What do they sell to buyers overseas?

4. What are some important advantages that an exporter may have that enable the company to compete with local firms in the target (importing) country?

THE XM COMPANY CASE (PART A)

Introduction

International trade takes place when companies either find new markets to sell their products in foreign countries or find new sources of supply of products in other countries. Exports and imports combined for the United States equal about 20% of GNP (gross national product), and the percentage is even higher for most other countries.

A very important factor in determining which countries will be able to compete in exporting different products is the cost of production. For example, if steel costs $300 per ton to make in Japan and $400 per ton to make in the United States, then U.S. customers should buy (import) steel from Japanese companies. By the same reasoning, if an airplane costs $4 million to build in the United States and $5 million in Japan, then Japanese customers should buy (import) airplanes from the United States. In this example, the United States produces and exports airplanes, while Japan produces and exports steel. Each country has a *comparative advantage* in producing one product relative to the other.

Obviously, countries do not export and import—*companies* do. A company should utilize comparative advantage to decide where to produce its products. In the case below, a U.S.-based company sells many products in several different national markets. The problem is to choose whether to obtain fertilizer in the United States or France, and perhaps to consider buying phosphate for resale as well.

The Case

XM Company is a Miami-based corporation involved in buying products from U.S. manufacturers for sale in Latin American and Caribbean countries. The company also finds U.S. markets for products imported from both Europe and Latin America. XM has twelve employees, including the general manager, a marketing vice president, a treasurer/controller, two sales managers, four operations people, and three secretaries. The firm's annual sales have run at about $5.7 million during the past three years, after growing from $200,000 in 1976, the first year of operations. Despite the various business-cycle problems that have occurred, this small firm has survived and is looking for ways to expand.

The general manager of XM is reviewing the profitable business that his company has had from importing fertilizers for central Florida farmers since the mid-1970s. The French supplier of XM's fertilizers (Agricosa) has always shipped high-quality merchandise, with few delays or other logistical problems. Recently, the possibility of competition from other suppliers has begun to worry the general manager. Fertilizer sales have been such a dependable part of XM's total sales that he does not want to lose that business.

Pricing, however, is becoming a problem. During the second major oil price hike in 1979–80, raw materials prices rose dramatically, such that XM's costs tripled by year-end 1981 to $120 per ton for its medium-grade fertilizer. This price reflects only the f.o.b. cost of the fertilizer at shipment from the port of Le Havre, France. Fortunately for XM, demand for fertilizer by the firm's main customers in central Florida has remained high, even at the higher prices that XM passed on.

Recently the company has been notified by the U.S. Treasury Department that fertilizers probably will be added to the list of products valued at the "American Selling Price" for customs purposes. (Under American Selling Price valuation, the tariff charged on an imported product is calculated as a percentage of the current *U.S. price*, rather than as a percentage of the stated price of the shipment.) Such a policy could raise the tariff payment significantly, because U.S. prices are about 15 percent higher than the f.o.b. price from France.

Competitive problems for XM have intensified since another French firm, Gardinier, set up a phosphate mine and processing facility near Tampa, Florida. Phosphates are a major component in most kinds of fertilizer. So far, Gardinier has been exporting the phosphates back to its French fertilizer plant, but it is expected that the company will soon begin making fertilizers in Florida. Gardinier ranks among the largest fertilizer producers in the world. At the present time, this French firm sees a cost of production of phosphates in Florida which undercuts the approximately $20 per ton cost in France by 30 percent. (All of these numbers are from 1981; the French franc has been devaluing relative to the dollar by about 8 percent per year during the last eight years.)

The general manager of XM is quite concerned by these developments in his fertilizer importing business, which constitutes 25 percent of XM's total sales. Though no major problems have arisen yet, the future looks rather clouded. Demand for fertilizer seems likely to remain substantial, but price competition is becoming an important factor.

COMPREHENSION QUESTIONS

Scanning

Scanning means reading very quickly in order to find key facts or figures that are contained within a text. Scan the case to determine whether the following statements are TRUE or FALSE.

_____ 1. XM Company is a large corporation located in Miami, Florida.

_____ 2. Agricosa supplies XM Company with fertilizer.

_____ 3. XM Company has been in operation since 1976.

_____ 4. XM had to pay three times as much for its medium-grade fertilizer in 1981 as it paid in 1980.

_____ 5. Fertilizers have already been added to the U.S. Treasury Department's list of products valued at the "American Selling Price."

_____ 6. Gardinier is selling fertilizer in Florida.

_____ 7. The general manager of XM is worried about the major competitive problems that his company is facing now in the fertilizer importing business.

_____ 8. Competition in fertilizer sales in Florida may come eventually from Gardinier.

Understanding Facts and Figures

The XM Company case presents many figures concerning annual sales, price increases, tariffs, and costs of production. Check your understanding of the numerical facts that you read in the case. Scan the case study to find the correct answers to the following questions.

1. What were the annual sales of the XM Company in 1976? What have their annual sales been over the past three years?

2. How many people are employed by XM Company?

3. How much did XM have to pay for medium-grade fertilizer after the 1979–80 oil price increase?

4. Explain what the effect would be of placing fertilizers on the list of products valued at the "American Selling Price" for customs purposes.

5. What percentage of XM Company's total sales comes from the fertilizer importing business?

Photo courtesy of the Florida Phosphate Council

VOCABULARY DEVELOPMENT

Word Guess

Readers often use contextual clues to help them understand the meaning of unfamiliar words. By looking at how the unknown word fits into the sentence and by examining the meaning of surrounding words, a reader can learn to make an educated guess about the meaning of the unknown word. Work on the valuable reading skill of guessing the meaning of unknown words by choosing the correct meaning of the underlined words.

1. The U.S. government charges a <u>tariff</u> on imports in order to protect goods produced in the United States. Typically, the <u>tariff</u> is equal to 20 percent of the current U.S. price for the product.

   a. tax

   b. price

   c. savings

2. The area around Tampa, Florida, is the site of several important phosphate mines. Phosphates are a major <u>component</u> of most fertilizers. Gardinier, one of the largest fertilizer producers in the world, operates a phosphate mine and processing facility near Tampa.

   a. part

   b. chemical

   c. example

3. Demand for phosphates is likely to remain <u>substantial</u> for the next decade, since fertilizer is an essential part of the agricultural industry worldwide.

   a. small

   b. superficial

   c. quite high

4. Gardinier <u>ranks among</u> the largest producers of fertilizer in the world. With its mine and processing plant in Florida, this French firm takes advantage of the lower cost of production of phosphates in the United States.

   a. sells to

   b. is one of the

   c. counts as its customers

5. The major oil price <u>hike</u> in 1979–80 caused the price of importing raw materials to rise by 200 percent. As a result, XM's costs tripled by the end of 1981.

   a. devaluation

   b. increase

   c. support

Determining Meaning from Context

Try to understand the meaning of the underlined words from their context, then explain the meaning in your own words to a partner. If you are not certain of the meaning, make a guess. Learning to determine the meaning of unfamiliar words from their context is a valuable skill that will help you to become more fluent in English.

1. When the cost of importing phosphates goes up, the XM Company has <u>to pass on the higher price</u> to its customers in order to make a profit.

   To pass on a higher price means to

2. The XM Company suffered during the difficult economic times of a few years ago. It survived the <u>business-cycle</u> problems and is looking for ways to expand its business.

   Business-cycle refers to

3. The cost of producing phosphates in Florida <u>undercuts</u> the cost of production in France by 30 percent. For this reason, Gardinier has set up a phosphate mine and processing plant near Tampa, Florida.

   To undercut is to

4. Fertilizer sales <u>constitute</u> an important part of XM Company's annual sales.

   To constitute means to

5. The XM Company increased the price of its <u>medium-grade</u> fertilizer by $100 per ton. The company also raised the price of its low-grade fertilizer.

   Medium-grade means

6. Imported products must pass through <u>customs</u> as they enter the country where they will be sold.

   Customs is

Vocabulary Building

You can increase your business vocabulary by learning to recognize the multiple forms of a word stem. For example, if you understand the word *competition*, you should recognize the related forms *competitive, to compete,* and *competitively*. Knowing how the word acts in the sentence will give you an even clearer understanding of its meaning. Fill in the chart with the appropriate forms of the commonly used business terms. Use a dictionary to check your answers, or exchange work with a partner to check his or her work.

Noun	Verb	Adjective	Adverb
competition			
supplier		(none)	(none)
logistics	(none)		
shipment			(none)
	devalue	(none)	(none)
			significantly
	intensify		

CRITICAL THINKING

Answer the following questions using the case description as a point of departure. You may work with a partner or a small group to prepare you answers.

1. Why do companies engage in international trade? Discuss some of opportunities and problems that multinational companies face.

2. Under what circumstances is exporting a certain product to another country profitable?

3. Give several examples of products that are exported from or imported to your country because of a comparative advantage.

4. Imagine that you are the manager of a new import-export firm in your country. What products will you trade? To which countries will you import or export these products? Give reasons for your choices.

5. What are some of the specific problems that you might encounter as manager of the import-export company in your country?

Photo courtesy of the Florida Phosphate Council

RESEARCH QUESTIONS

To answer these questions you will need to conduct research outside of the classroom. In your search for the answers, you may want to contact local businessmen and -women, the chamber of commerce, government officials, or a library. Work with a partner or a small group to determine how and where to find the information, and share your findings. When you are finished, present the results of your research in a brief summary to the class.

1. What percentage of your country's gross national product (GNP) comes from exports and imports?

2. What products are the principal exports of your country? The principal imports?

3. Contact the manager of an import-export firm. Prepare a list of questions to ask her or him concerning the company's products, where the goods are exported to or imported from, the size of the company, and opportunities and challenges in running the company. Ask other questions that you feel are appropriate. Summarize the manager's responses for your group or the class.

4. Find an article in a current English-language newspaper or magazine about any aspect of the import-export business. Read the article and be prepared to summarize it for your group or the class. Your summary should be brief, no longer than three minutes in length. Mention only the main points of the article. For your pre-

Photo by Christine U. Grosse

sentation, try not to read the summary from notes. Instead, organize your thoughts before you present your findings.

CASE ANALYSIS

The general manager of the XM Company has asked you and the other officers of the firm to review the profitability of the fertilizer business. In addition, he has requested that you recommend ways to expand the company's operations in the United States and abroad. You should consider how price competition may affect the fertilizer business in the future as you plan a strategy for the company to follow.

In your case analysis, discuss the questions below with the other members of your group. Then make the appropriate recommendations to the manager of XM Company.

1. How important is the fertilizer business to the XM Company? What other business should the company consider entering?

2. What is the level of demand for the fertilizer in central Florida? Is the demand likely to change over the next few years?

3. Describe how the pricing of the fertilizer is becoming a problem for XM Company. Consider the effect of the changing cost of:

   a. oil

   b. raw materials

   c. U.S. tariff on imported fertilizers

4. Describe the competitive problems that XM Company may face from Gardinier, considering the following points:

   a. What operations has Gardinier set up in Florida?

   b. What impact have these operations had on XM's fertilizer business?

   c. What is the comparative advantage of producing fertilizers in the United States rather than France? What possible effect could this have on XM's fertilizer business?

5. Based on your discussion of these issues, make recommendations on how to expand XM's fertilizer business and how to increase profitability.

2

THE XM COMPANY CASE (PART B)

Protecting against exchange risk

Photo by Christine U. Grosse

PREREADING EXERCISE

Discuss the following questions before reading the case study.

1. What does "risk" mean?

2. What kinds of risk are involved when a company does business in a foreign country?

3. What is an exchange rate? How are exchange rates determined?

4. How can exchange rates present risks to international corporations?

THE XM COMPANY CASE (PART B)

Introduction

Foreign-exchange risk is a major concern to managers of companies involved in international business. This risk exists whenever the company has to make or accept a payment in a foreign currency. The risk exists because the number of dollars (for U.S. firms) or pesos (for Mexican firms) or yen (for Japanese firms) in a contract may vary if the account is payable or receivable in foreign currency and the exchange rate changes. For example, a contract by XM Company calls for payment of 1 million yen in 180 days to buy computer chips. Today, the exchange rate is 200 yen per dollar, so the contract would cost $5000 if paid today. If the dollar devalues to a rate of 167 yen per dollar in 180 days, then the cost of the contract would be $6000 in 180 days. We cannot know the dollar cost of the contract for sure until time passes and the new exchange rate is known. The possible devaluation of the dollar creates an exchange-rate risk that the firm would like to avoid.

Exchange risk can be avoided by doing business only in the company's domestic currency. This possibility often does not exist, because the foreign customer or supplier has other choices of suppliers or customers who *will* deal in the foreign currency. U.S. firms doing business in Germany usually have to work in German marks (DM) rather than dollars. Similarly, if a U.S. supplier in Brazil will not accept local currency (*cruzeiros*, abbreviated Cr$*) for a sale, then the Brazilian buyer may find a German or Japanese firm that will. Thus, this strategy of risk avoidance often does not work.

---

*A new Brazilian currency, the cruzado, was issued in 1985. The conversion rate is 1 cruzado = 1000 cruzeiros.

Another strategy to cope with foreign-exchange risk is to use a *forward contract*. A forward contract is an agreement with a bank to exchange one currency for another at some future date at a price chosen today. Most multinational banks offer forward contracts to clients using the major trading currencies (such as the U.S. dollar, German mark, Swiss franc, French franc, British pound, and Canadian dollar). In the example above, the XM Company can ask a bank for a forward contract to buy 1 million yen in 180 days. This contract would enable XM to guarantee that it will have the 1 million yen needed to pay for the computer chips in 180 days at a known price, the *forward rate*. If the forward rate is 182 yen per dollar, then XM knows that the cost will be $5495 in 180 days. By using a forward contract with a bank, XM avoids exchange risk; the number of dollars to be paid for the computer chips is known from the start.

A third way to avoid exchange risk is to attempt to balance the company's accounts payable and accounts receivable in each currency used. For example, the company may try to make a sale in the same currency in which it already has an account payable. That way, when the payment is made, a receipt in the same currency will be obtained, approximately canceling the risk that existed. In a previous case, the XM Company bought fertilizer from a French company. In order to eliminate the exchange risk due to having an account payable in French francs. XM could attempt to find French customers for some product that it would export from the United States to France. XM would receive French francs for this sale, to balance the francs payable to its fertilizer supplier.

Several other methods are available to cope with exchange risk. Again, in the event that the firm has an account payable in foreign exchange, it may look for some other asset such as a bank deposit or another investment that is payable at the same date and in the same currency as the account payable for the same amount of money. Or, if the firm has an account receivable in some currency, it can take out a loan for the same time period and amount of money in that currency. In every case, the goal is to find some asset (to cancel a liability) or some liability (to cancel an asset) denominated in the same currency with the same maturity date. In this way, exchange risk can be avoided. The process of protecting against exchange-rate risk is called *hedging* or *covering*.

The Case

The financial manager of XM Company in Miami has been bothered by a relatively low return (in dollars) on his export sales to Brazil since 1978. XM's sales office in São Paulo has experienced a healthy growth of revenues at about 15 percent per year, though local-currency (cruzeiro) profits have only grown by 12 percent per year. (Cruzeiro profits were Cr$500 million in 1983.) Also, the cruzeiro has devalued substantially relative to the dollar. At the end of 1978 the exchange rate was Cr$21 = US$1, but in January of 1984 the rate was Cr$1200 = US$1, and the trend seemed likely to continue.

Having some familiarity with foreign-exchange markets, the financial manager has decided to cover his next contract (that is, protect it against exchange-rate risk), which is a sale of Cr$30 million of tractor parts, payable in 180 days, to a firm in São Paulo. Despite calls to several banks in Miami and Brazil, he could not obtain a forward contract for cruzeiros. He did, however, discover that a local-currency loan was available to cover the full receivable at a cost of 105 percent per year. At this time, he was not certain whether any other cruzeiro liability was available to create the hedge.

In a separate transaction, a purchase of DM 250,000 worth of agricultural chemicals will be imported from the German company Bayer Chemical in 120 days. The financial manager wants to plan now to have sufficient funds available to pay this bill on time. He knows that the spot exchange rate is DM1 = $0.416, and that the forward rate for a 120-day contract is DM1 = $0.421 in Miami. Considering "riskless" securities in which to hold the funds until needed, the manager finds that 120-day U.S. Treasury bills offer 8.5 percent per year, while West German Central Bank bills offer 7.1 percent per year. The manager was satisfied with this information as a basis for making his decision to hedge the risk in German marks.

As he reflects on the foreign-exchange problem in each of the transactions above, XM's financial manager sees a serious inefficiency in his piecemeal approach to risk avoidance. At present, however, he sees no easy solution.

COMPREHENSION QUESTIONS

Scanning

Read the following statements and mark them TRUE or FALSE. Reword the false statements so that they are true. Scan the case description to confirm your answers.

_____ 1. A Japanese company can avoid exchange risk by dealing only in yen.

_____ 2. Managers of companies that are engaged in international business must cope with foreign-exchange risk.

U.S. FOREIGN EXCHANGE MARKETS

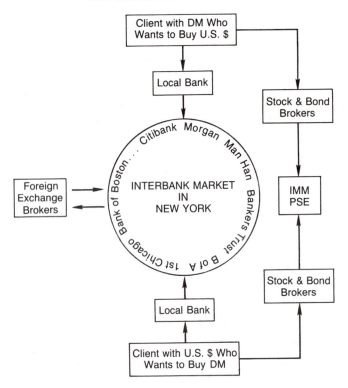

_____ 3. Foreign-exchange risk exists when a contract is payable or receivable in a foreign currency and the exchange rate for that currency is variable.

_____ 4. Company managers usually know how much the rate of exchange for a foreign currency will vary over a period of time.

_____ 5. A forward contract is an agreement with a bank to exchange one currency for another at some time in the future at the spot rate of exchange.

Read for Understanding of Key Concepts

Answer the following questions on the basis of your reading of the case description. Scan the text to find the information that you need.

1. Explain how a company can use a forward contract to avoid exchange-rate risk.

2. Give examples of how a company can avoid exchange risk by balancing accounts payable with accounts receivable.

3. What is *hedging*? Why do companies do it?

4. Is the sale of tractor parts to a firm in São Paulo an account receivable or an account payable for the XM Company?

5. Is the purchase of agricultural chemicals from the Bayer Company in West Germany an account payable or an account receivable for the XM Company?

6. What is the trend in the exchange rate of U.S. dollars for Brazilian cruzeiros?

VOCABULARY DEVELOPMENT

Sentence Completion

Demonstrate your understanding of the underlined business phrases by completing the sentences below with your own words. Work with a partner and take turns doing the exercise. Refer to the case description for clarification of any terms that are unfamiliar.

1. An import-export company can avoid foreign-exchange risk by

2. One of the reasons that a company buys riskless securities is

3. A forward contract guarantees that

4. Hedging against foreign-exchange risk means

5. The accounts payable of a company often include

6. In a forward contract, the forward rate is

7. The forward rate is typically _____ than the spot exchange rate because

Matching

The business terms below are used in the case description. Match the terms with their correct meanings. Refer to the case description when you are in doubt about the meanings of any words. Compare your answers with those of another student and discuss any discrepancies.

_____ 1. foreign exchange   a. income from an investment

_____ 2. maturity date   b. account receivable

_____ 3. revenue   c. covering

_____ 4. liability   d. when payment is due

_____ 5. asset   e. trade in currencies

_____ 6. hedging   f. possibility of losing money

_____ 7. risk   g. account payable

_____ 8. riskless security   h. U.S. Treasury bill

Business Terminology: Assets and Liabilities

Decide whether the following financial terms refer to an ASSET or a LIABILITY. Remember that an asset is a balance-sheet item such as cash, accounts receivable, inventories, and plant and equipment. A liability represents the obligations of a firm, such as accounts payable, notes payable, long-term debt, and taxes due.

1. 30,000 tractors _____

2. a loan of $400,000 _____

3. a bank deposit of DM6,000,000 _____

4. $1,000 U.S. Treasury bill _____

5. a forward contract to pay 10,000 yen in 120

   days _____

6. a contract to buy DM20,000 worth of chemicals _____

Currencies

Name the local currency of the following countries.

1. France _____

2. Brazil _____

3. West Germany _____

4. United States _____

5. Japan _____

Photo by Christine U. Grosse

6. Great Britain _____

7. Mexico _____

8. Saudi Arabia _____

9. Spain _____

10. Switzerland _____

CRITICAL THINKING

Analysis of Issues

Think carefully about the following questions concerning issues discussed in the case descriptions. Share your ideas with a partner or a small group. Be prepared to explain your answers to the class.

1. According to the case, the XM Company has received a fairly low return in dollars on export sales to Brazil over the past few years. However, the sales office of XM in São Paulo has increased its revenues by about 15 percent per year. Explain how XM's profits in dollars can be considered low under these circumstances. Begin by explaining the difference between profit and revenue.

2. What is the value in dollars of the tractor parts?

3. What is the interest rate of the local-currency loan that is available

to the XM Company in Brazil? What percentage interest would be charged during the 180-day period of the loan?

4. Why isn't a forward contract available in cruzeiros?

5. In order to avoid exchange-rate risk, should the XM Company buy a U.S. Treasury bill or a West German Central Bank bill? Explain the reason for your answer.

6. Are the two transactions described in the case linked in any way? Explain your answer.

Money Market Hedge

As general manager of XM Company, you want to use a money-market hedge to protect the company against exchange-rate risk in the two transactions described in the case. You need to think about the questions below in order to perform the hedge. Use the formulas provided for your calculations. You may work alone or with a partner.

1. I want to take out a loan in cruzeiros to balance our account receivable for the tractor parts. How many cruzeiros should I borrow today so that my debt will be Cr$30,000,000 in 180 days?

Use this formula:

$$\frac{\text{cruzeiros receivable for tractor parts}}{1 \ + \ \text{interest rate}} = \text{amount of loan today}$$

(Remember to calculate the interest rate for 180 days.)

But I still have exchange-rate risk until I exchange the cruzeiros for dollars. So how many dollars do I need to exchange today to take the loan in cruzeiros?

2. I need a deutsche mark (DM) asset that will be worth DM250,000 in 120 days. How much will I need to invest today in a West German Central Bank bill so that it will be worth DM250,000 in 120 days?

Use this formula:

$$\frac{\text{amount payable for chemicals in 120 days}}{1 \ + \ \text{interest rate}} = \text{amount to invest today}$$

(Remember that the interest rate is for 120 days.)

What is the cost of this investment in dollars?

RESEARCH QUESTIONS

Find the answers to the following questions by doing research outside the classroom. You may find it helpful to work with several classmates as you conduct the research necessary to carry out the assignments. The sources of the information you seek include an international bank, an import-export company, and an English-language magazine or newspaper article.

1. Through the telephone directory or local chamber of commerce, identify a bank that offers forward contracts. Find out in which currencies the contracts are available, for what periods of time they are issued, and at what rates. Then compare the forward-contract rate for each currency wth the spot exchange rate.

2. Again using the telephone book or a list supplied by the chamber of commerce, call an import-export company in your area. Find out how the company avoids foreign-exchange risk. Ask for specific examples of how the firm protects itself against exchange-rate risk.

3. Look for a recent article on changes in foreign-exchange rates and the impact on business. You may find a suitable article in *Business Week, Euromoney, Forbes*, or *The Wall Street Journal*.

CASE ANALYSIS

You are part of a team whose assignment is to develop a plan to manage the foreign-exchange risk of the XM Company. Your group will evaluate the proposals listed below in order to decide which are the best ways to avoid exchange risk. After you have weighed each alternative, you will make recommendations to the general manager of XM Company concerning which course of action to follow. Be prepared to defend your decision.

Sale of Tractor Parts to Brazil

Options for avoiding exchange-rate risk

1. Take a loan now that will be worth Cr$30 million in four months.

2. Borrow $30 million from a U.S. bank.

3. Buy Cr$30 million worth of coffee to import to the United States, payable in six months.

4. Sell the account receivable for the tractor parts at a discount that XM Company can collect in six months.

5. Deposit Cr$30 million in a Brazilian bank account.

Purchase of Agricultural Chemicals from Bayer Company

Options for avoiding exchange-rate risk

1. Buy a U.S. Treasury bill worth DM250,000 in four months.

2. Purchase a West German Central Bank bill worth DM250,000 in 120 days.

3. Export DM250,000 worth of computers from the United States to West Germany, receivable in 120 days.

4. Take a loan of DM250,000, payable in 120 days.

5. Take a forward contract that is worth DM250,000 180 days from now.

3

THE AMERITECH CORPORATION CASE

Cultural differences in business practices

Photo courtesy of the Ministry of Information, Bahrain, from the brochure "Bahrain"

PREREADING EXERCISE

Discuss the following questions in class before reading the case.

1. Is it an acceptable business practice to pay a fee to a government official who assists your company in arranging a business deal? Why or why not?

2. Is it an acceptable business practice to pay a fee to a company offical who assists your company in arranging a business deal? Why or why not?

3. The U.S. government passed the Foreign Corrupt Practices Act in 1977. The law forbids companies to pay foreign officials for the purpose of influencing any business or business-related decision. What effect has this had on American business?

4. Are government employees allowed to work in private business at the same time in your country? How might this complicate business decisions?

THE AMERITECH CORPORATION CASE

Introduction

Ameritech is one of the four largest U.S. firms that produce military and commercial aircraft and highly sophisticated electronic equipment for the navigation of airplanes, rockets, and missiles. For the past forty-five years, the firm has been selling most of its products to the U.S. government, governments of friendly countries, and commercial airlines. The national airlines of more than a dozen countries use Ameritech planes in their fleets.

During the past five years a recession has plagued most of the Third World, after crippling the industrialized countries during 1981–83. As seen in Ameritech's income statement (Table 3–1), sales in Latin America and the Middle East account for about 26 percent of the total business of the firm. These sales have dropped dramatically since 1980, and consequently Ameritech has faced reduced revenues during this time period.

The Case

Mr. John Williams, Ameritech's sales manager in the Middle East, was considering a problem that had arisen last week in his negotiations for the sale of five commerical jets to the government of Bahrain. Ameritech had not previously done business with this coun-

TABLE 3–1   Ameritech Corporation 1984 Income Statement *(in millions)*

Sales, according to geographic segment	
North America	$3700
Europe	1500
Latin America	1200
Middle East	700
Asia and other	400
Total sales	7500
Other income	200
Total income	7700
Cost of goods sold	(6400)
Administrative and overhead costs	(600)
Interest expense	(50)
Net income before tax	650
Taxes paid	(270)
Net income after tax	380

TABLE 3–2   Ameritech Corporation Balance Sheet, Year-end 1984 *(in millions of U.S. dollars)*

ASSETS		LIABILITIES	
Cash, etc.	30	Accrued wages and salaries	230
Accounts receivable	720	Accounts payable	610
Inventories	1300	Notes payable	250
		Taxes payable	380
Property, plant, and equipment	1100	Long-term debt	120
Other assets	150	Shareholders' equity	1710
Total assets	3300	Total liabilities plus shareholders' equity	3300

try. Until last year, Bahrain had purchased only from Airbus Industries, the joint French-British company. Because of some dissatisfaction with Airbus, which had failed to service its planes as quickly as contracted, Bahrain's government was seeking bids from other aircraft manufacturers.

Ameritech responded to the request from Bahrain with a carefully prepared proposal. The firm undoubtedly would be able to meet the conditions specified in its proposed service contract. In fact, superior service was one of the competitive strengths of Ameritech relative to its main competitors. It was expected that the prices quoted by each bidder would be about equal, and that all the bidders could deliver the planes within two years.

In his attempts to find an influential person to serve as agent for Ameritech in negotiations with the government, Mr. Williams had encountered an American-educated local businessman named Ahmed Rashad. Mr. Rashad once worked for the Ministry of Transportation. Since the Ministry would be the official purchaser of the airplanes, it appeared to Mr. Williams that an arrangement with Mr. Rashad would be very valuable.

Mr. Williams found that his discussions with Mr. Rashad were open and encouraging. After only three meetings, Mr. Rashad agreed to accept a consultant's fee of $100,000 from Ameritech in exchange for his efforts to convince the government to buy the planes from the firm. This consulting arrangement was quite normal for major project negotiations in Bahrain. Ameritech had previously used former military and government officials as consultants in the United States and elsewhere in its business.

As negotiations proceeded, Mr. Williams discovered that his choice of Mr. Rashad had been a good one. Ameritech ultimately became one of the three finalists in bidding to supply the aircraft. The previous week Mr. Rashad came to him with the exciting news that the Transportation Minister had confided that Ameritech would probably be chosen very soon as the winner. In addition to that news, Mr. Rashad explained that a payment of $500,000 would be viewed as an acceptable fee to pay the Minister for his consideration of the bid. This payment would be added to Mr. Rashad's fee and paid to him.

Now Mr. Williams was in a difficult position. He was aware that the additional payment was common in deals such as this one, and that Ameritech had always played by the rules required in each country where the firm did business. However, since the Foreign Corrupt Practices Act of 1977, things had changed for American firms. Ameritech would have to declare the $500,000 payment (to Mr. Rashad) as a consulting fee, and it would be scrutinized by the U.S. Justice Department very carefully to judge its legality. (The appendix to this case cites relevant parts of the Foreign Corrupt Practices Act.) The payment could be construed as a bribe, and then both he and the company would be penalized. Mr. Williams was unsure whether or not to proceed with the deal.

Mr. Williams knew that the other two finalists in the bidding were Airbus Industries and a Japanese consortium of aircraft manufacturers. He was sure that they would not hesitate to pay the additional fee. In fact, he felt angry that the U.S. government was "punishing" American firms by requiring them to meet the terms of the Act, while foreign competitors faced no such limitations. He was virtually certain that the contract would be lost if he did not go along with the request for additional payment.

APPENDIX

Foreign Corrupt Practices Act of 1977

Sec. 104. (a) It shall be unlawful for any domestic concern, other than an issuer which is subject to section 30A of the Securities Exchange Act of 1934, or any officer, director, employee, or agent of such domestic concern or any stockholder thereof acting on behalf of such domestic concern, to make use of the mails or any means or instrumentality of interstate commerce corruptly in the furtherance of an offer, payment, promise to pay, or authorization of the giving of value to

(1) any foreign official for purposes of (A) influencing any act or decision of such foreign official in his official capacity, including a decision to fail to perform his official functions; or (B) inducing such foreign official to use his influence with a foreign government or instrumentality thereof to affect or influence any act or decision of such government or instrumentality, in order to assist such domestic concern in obtaining or retaining business for or with, or directing business to, any person;

(2) any foreign political party or official thereof or any candidate for foreign political office for purposes of (A) influencing any act or decision of such party, official or candidate in its or his official capacity, including a decision to fail to perform its or his official functions; or (B) inducing such party, official, or candidate to use its or his influence with a foreign government or instrumentality thereof to affect or influence any act or decision of such government or instrumentality, in order to assist such domestic concern in obtaining or retaining business for or with, or directing business to, any person; or

(3) any person, while knowing or having reason to know that all or a portion of such money or thing of value will be offered, given, or promised, directly or indirectly, to any foreign official, to any foreign political party or official thereof, or to any candidate for foreign political office, for purposes of (A) influencing any act or decision of such foreign official, political party, party official, or candidate in his or its official capacity, including a decision to fail to perform his or its official functions; or (B) inducing such foreign official, political party, party official, or candidate to use his or its influence with a foreign government or instrumentality thereof to affect or influence any act or decision of such government or instrumentality, in order to assist such domestic concern in obtaining or retaining business for or with, or directing business to, any person.

(b) (1) (A) Except as provided in subparagraph (B), any domestic concern which violates subsection (a) shall, upon conviction, be fined not more than $1,000,000.

(B) Any individual who is a domestic concern and who willfully violates subsection (a) shall, upon conviction, be fined not more than $10,000, or imprisoned not more than five years, or both.

(2) Any officer or director of a domestic concern, or stockholder acting on behalf of such domestic concern, who willfully violates subsection (a) shall, upon conviction, be fined not more than $10,000, or imprisoned not more than five years, or both.

(3) Whenever a domestic concern is found to have violated subsection (a) of this section, any employee or agent of such domestic concern who is a United States citizen, national, or resident or is otherwise subject to the jurisdiction of the United States (other than an officer, director, or stockholder acting on behalf of such domestic concern) and who willfully carried out the practice constituting such violation shall, upon conviction, be fined not more than $10,000, or imprisoned not more than five years, or both.

(4) Whenever a fine is imposed under paragraph (2) or (3) of this subsection upon any officer, director, stockholder, employee, or agent of a domestic concern, such fine shall not be paid, directly or indirectly, by such domestic concern.

(c) Whenever it appears to the Attorney General that any domestic concern, or officer, director, employee, agent, or stockholder thereof, is engaged, or is about to engage, in any act or practice constituting a violation of subsection (a) of this section, the Attorney General may, in his discretion, bring a civil action in an appropriate district court of the United States to enjoin such act or practice, and upon a proper showing a permanent or temporary injunction or a temporary restraining order shall be granted without bond.

(d) As used in this section:

(1) The term "domestic concern" means (A) any individual who is a citizen, national, or resident of the United States; or (B) any corporation, partnership, association, joint-stock company, business trust, unincorporated organization, or sole proprietorship which has its principal place of business in the United States, or which is organized under the laws of a State of the United States or a territory, possession, or commonwealth of the United States.

(2) The term "foreign official" means any officer or employee of a foreign government or any department, agency, or instrumentality thereof, or any person acting in an official capacity for or on behalf of any such government or department, agency, or instrumentality. Such term does not include any employee of a foreign government or any department, agency, or instrumentality thereof whose duties are essentially ministerial or clerical.

(3) The term "interstate commerce" means trade, commerce, transportation, or communication among the several States, or between any foreign country and any State, or between any State and any place or ship outside thereof. Such term includes the interstate use of (A) a telephone or other interstate means of communication, or (B) any other interstate instrumentality.

Photo courtesy of Eastern Airlines

COMPREHENSION QUESTIONS

Understanding the Main Idea

Refer to the case description if necessary to answer the following questions. Scan the text for the information you need.

1. What does Ameritech produce?

2. Who are Ameritech's major clients?

3. What is the general financial condition of the company?

4. Describe the deal that Mr. Williams is negotiating in Bahrain.

5. Why is Bahrain seeking bids for the project?

6. Who is Mr. Rashad?

7. What is Mr. Rashad's consulting arrangement with Ameritech?

8. Why is Mr. Williams concerned about the payment of $500,000 to the Minister of Transportation?

9. Who were the other two finalists in the bidding for the contract?

10. Is Mr. Williams confident that his company will win the bid? Give reasons for your answer.

Scanning for Factual Information

Glance quickly over the Foreign Corrupt Practices Act in order to find the information necessary to complete the following exercises.

1. What is a domestic concern?

2. According to the Foreign Corrupt Practices Act, what behavior is unlawful for domestic concerns?

3. What does the term "interstate commerce" refer to here?

4. Who is considered to be a "foreign official" according to this Act? To whom does the term *not* refer?

5. What is the maximum amount that a company could be fined for violating the Act?

6. How long could an individual be imprisoned for violating the Act?

Scanning an Income Statement for Facts and Figures

Briefly look over the Ameritech Corporation 1984 income statement (Table 3–1) to find the answers to these questions.

1. In what part of the world did Ameritech make its greatest sales?

2. Compare the company sales in the Middle East with those in Latin America.

3. What expenses did the company have?

4. What was the company's net income after tax?

Interpreting a Balance Sheet

Examine the Ameritech balance sheet (Table 3–2) in order to give an opinion on whether the financial condition of the company is good or bad. Consider the following questions as you make your judgment.

1. How many millions of dollars does the company have in liquid assets?

2. What marketable securities does the company possess?

3. What short-term debts must the company pay?

4. Will the company be able to pay the short-term debt? How might it do this?

VOCABULARY DEVELOPMENT

Word Derivatives

Many words in English are derived from the same root. The suffixes that are attached to the root, such as *-er*, *-tion*, *-ry*, and *-al*, provide clues to the meaning and usage of the word. Discuss how the words are used and the meaning of the suffixes. Then select the appropriate word to complete each sentence below.

　produces
　producer
　production
　products

1. The Japanese firm ＿＿＿＿＿＿ highly sophisticated electronic equipment.

2. ＿＿＿＿＿＿ of commercial aircraft decreased during the recession.

3. Ameritech Corporation is a leading ＿＿＿＿＿＿ of military aircraft.

4. Bahrain agreed to buy several ＿＿＿＿＿＿ from the European company.

　purchases
　purchase
　purchaser

1. In spite of the high cost, the government decided to ＿＿＿＿＿＿ the navigational instruments.

2. After months of negotiations, the aircraft company found a ＿＿＿＿＿＿ for its new missile.

3. The businessman made numerous ＿＿＿＿＿＿ on his trip to Bahrain.

　bribes
　bribe
　bribery

1. The Minister of Transportation did not ask directly for a ＿＿＿＿＿＿ .

2. In spite of the Foreign Corrupt Practices Act, the businessman attempted to _____ the government official.

3. In 1977 the U.S. Justice Department passed a law against the _____ of foreign officials for the purpose of doing business.

    contracts
    contract
    contractor
    contractual

1. Ameritech submitted a bid to become the _____ for the project.

2. After six months of negotiations, the government decided to _____ with the Japanese firm.

3. The company failed to honor its _____ to service the aircraft.

4. The _____ agreement stated that all repairs would be made within thirty days.

    consult
    consultant
    consultation
    consulting

1. As _____ to the project, Mr. Rashad requested a fee of $100,000.

2. The company considered it necessary to _____ with Mr. Rashad about the sale of the aircraft.

3. In _____ with Mr. Rashad, the firm raised its bid for the project.

4. According to the U.S. government, the _____

   arrangement was not legal.

   bids

   bid

   bidding

   bidder

1. Frequently the contract is awarded to the highest

   _____.

2. When the Japanese company decided to submit a _____

   for the project, the American competitor began to worry.

3. Finally the Dutch firm entered the _____ to supply the

   aircraft.

4. Five companies _____ for the project.

Sentence Completion: Use of the Passive in Conditional Sentences

The passive form of verbs can be used to express possibility in conditional sentences. Complete the following sentences by describing an appropriate condition. Scan the case if you need to find information to complete the sentences.

1. The minister confided that Ameritech would probably be chosen as the winner, since

2. The payment of $500,000 would be added to the fee of Mr. Rashad for

3. Mr. Williams knew that the consulting fee would be scrutinized carefully by the U.S. Justice Department, because

4. The payment could be construed as a bribe because

5. The company and Mr. Williams would be penalized if

6. Other companies bidding for the project would probably not be constrained by the need to pay the additional fee, since

7. Mr. Williams was certain that the contract would be lost if

Photo courtesy of the Ministry of Information, Bahrain, from the brochure "Bahrain"

CRITICAL THINKING

Work on the following questions with a partner. Exchange ideas and information in order to discover answers to the questions.

1. What is Mr. Williams's biggest problem in negotiating a contract with the government of Bahrain? Why is it a problem?

2. Skim the Foreign Corrupt Practices Act. How do its rules apply to the case?

3. In your opinion, is the $500,000 payment to the Minister of Transportation a bribe? Give reasons for your answer. Discuss the conditions in which a consultant's fee is earned, and when it is a bribe.

4. The Ameritech Corporation case focuses on cultural differences and attitudes. Discuss other cultural differences that can lead to problems in doing business. (For example, you might consider different concepts of time, styles of management, expected behavior, or language barriers.)

5. How important are ethics in doing business? What kinds of behavior in business are considered unethical in your country? Does

Photo courtesy of the Ministry of Information, Bahrain, from the brochure "Bahrain"

the definition of "unethical" behavior vary from country to country?

RESEARCH QUESTIONS

The following questions require that you conduct research outside of the classroom in order to find the answers. Work with a partner or a small group to complete the assignments.

1. Identify an office of a large U.S. corporation in your area from the telephone directory or the local chamber of commerce. Speak with the public-relations officer about how the company's business practices abroad have been affected by the Foreign Corrupt Practices Act of 1977.

2. Talk with representatives from two multinational firms that have headquarters in different countries. Again, use the phone book or the directory of the chamber of commerce to identify the firms. Interview the firms' business personnel about how they view the role of bribes in doing business. Are bribes a common and accepted part of business in some areas of the world? Where? Compare the views of the two companies.

3. Find an article in an English-language magazine or newspaper that deals with corruption or bribery in international business. Prepare a summary of the main ideas of the article. Who is it about? When and where do the events of the article take place?

What are the major implications of the news story? Be prepared to give a three-minute oral summary to the class.

CASE ANALYSIS

You are a member of a team of consultants working for Ameritech. Discuss the key issues that are involved in winning the contract for aircraft production for Bahrain. How will the government decide who will be awarded the contract?

In view of the Minister's request for a fee, how should Ameritech proceed? Consider the question from the following points of view:

1. The legal aspect

What is a legal solution to the case? Base your argument on your knowledge of the Foreign Corrupt Practices Act.

2. The moral aspect

What is a possible moral solution to the case? Compare and contrast the legal and moral solutions to the issue.

4

THE MONSTER CHOMP COOKIES CASE

International marketing

Photo courtesy of the Brazilian Government Trade Bureau

PREREADING EXERCISE

Discuss the following questions in class before reading the case.

1. What is your favorite commercial (on television) or advertisement (in a magazine or newspaper)? What in particular do you like about it?

2. What can a company do to promote a new product?

3. When a company wants to market in another country a food product that was successful in the home country, what cultural differences does it have to take into consideration?

4. In your country, how do companies promote snack foods such as cookies and crackers?

THE MONSTER CHOMP COOKIES CASE

Introduction

Marketing managers in international business must cope with a great variety of conditions abroad that differ from those at home. Consumers' tastes (literally) often differ from one country to the next; packaging may need to be altered; distribution channels frequently must be changed because of different costs and availabilities; pricing may need to be adjusted to local market conditions; and promotional strategy may have to change because of language and media. In all, the marketing function is subject to many very important differences when a firm chooses to do business in another country.

In the food industry, many companies have discovered major difficulties in expanding distribution of their successful products from the home country into other national markets. Campbell's soup, for example, had tremendous problems entering the European market because of the taste of its products. Campbell's had to change the flavor of its soups (especially tomato soup) to attract European customers. Knorr soups, originally introduced in European countries, suffered very low sales when first sold in the United States, because the soup is dehydrated and American consumers prefer to buy soup in liquid form. But Knorr has persisted with its dried soups, and over the years has developed a large-enough market segment to justify operating in the United States.

This case was written by Professor Robert Grosse as a basis for class discussion. Background materials were provided by Beatrice Companies, Inc. Any errors are the responsibility of the author.

When a language difference exists, the company must deal with the need to translate its promotional statements and any other explanatory materials that accompany the product. This problem can be particularly frustrating: The Chevrolet division of General Motors Corporation lost a lot of money trying to sell its popular Nova model in Puerto Rico before discovering that "Nova" meant "won't go" in Spanish. Similarly, an international airline used the company name EMU in Australia before discovering that an emu is an Australian bird that cannot fly. Even Pepsi-Cola ran into trouble with translation when it used the advertisement "Come alive with Pepsi" in Germany; in German the ad meant "Come back from the grave with Pepsi." As these three examples demonstrate, the problem of translation may present a major hurdle for the firm that wants to enter a foreign market.

An additional concern that should be taken very seriously when entering a less developed country is that, even beyond language and tastes, business is carried out differently in different cultural settings. For example, most sales of food products in Latin America traditionally have been made in small corner stores or open-air markets, not in supermarkets. Storage space generally is quite small, so food-processing firms must make frequent (once or twice a week)

Photo courtesy of the Brazilian Government Trade Bureau

deliveries to the stores. This contrast with the less-frequent, large-volume deliveries to supermarkets in the United States. (Despite this historical fact, a 1983 survey of Brazilian food-purchasing habits showed that 68 percent of total food sales were taking place in supermarkets at that time. Apparently, buying patterns are becoming more like those in the United States.)

Each of these concerns was relevant when Beatrice Companies, a major U.S. food-processing firm, sought to enter the highly competitive Brazilian market for cookies.

The Case

Beatrice Companies, Inc., is a highly diversified producer of processed foods, beverages, consumer products, chemicals, and other products in thirty countries, with sales offices and licensees in more than 120 more. Annual sales in 1984 were about $12 billion worldwide, with about three-fourths of that in the United States. Less than 5 percent of the company's sales occur in Latin America, although Beatrice is a market leader in most products it sells in the region.

Beatrice entered the Brazilian market through acquisition of 80 percent ownership in an existing local firm, Ailiram, S.A., in 1983. Ailiram was a local manufacturer of cookies and candies in the State of São Paulo, selling mainly to small retail stores outside of the city of São Paulo. Ailiram's cookies were very similar to those sold by dozens of other Brazilian firms—plain, fairly undifferentiated, round cookies and biscuits made of wheat flour and sugar. (They are often called "Maria cookies.") The company, formed in 1945, had grown to include two manufacturing plants and over 1000 employees by 1983. Beatrice intended to use Ailiram as a base for entering the national market in Brazil, first by pursuing supermarket sales in the city of São Paulo, then by expanding product lines and distribution throughout the whole country.

Soon after the acquisition, managers of the subsidiary were planning a strategy to break into the highly competitive market for sales of cookies to supermarkets. A survey of the market showed that about a dozen other companies already sold similar products to leading supermarkets. Table 4–1 is a market survey of cookie sales in São Paulo and Rio de Janeiro in 1984. Ailiram calculated that it would have very little chance to displace any of them unless it produced a differentiated product (that is, a different type of cookie).

On a trip to the United States, one Ailiram executive noticed the highly successful "Monster Chomp" cookies sold there. She felt that this product had good potential for sales in Brazil, since such unusual cookies were not available there. Ailiram's attempt to sell to supermarkets would be enhanced greatly by the appealing packages of "Monstrinho Creck" cookies. They would sell at the top end of the cookie market, where only two or three other brands were competing. By successfully selling Monstrinho Creck cookies, Ailiram would (1) establish an image of high-quality, innovative products and (2) gain access to supermarkets. Both of these were goals set by Beatrice, which wanted to compete nationally throughout Brazil in both the cookie and candy markets.

Biscuits (that is, Maria cookies) are probably the most widely distributed product in Brazil, as they are often the only thing eaten for breakfast. In terms of total volume, the supermarkets account for over 60 percent of sales of food products in general and these cookies in particular.

In the United States, Monster Chomps were soft cookies, much thicker and softer than the cookies sold normally in Brazil. Ailiram's managers felt that cookies had to be hard and flat in order to meet Brazilian children's tastes, but the shape could be unusual. Thus, it was decided to produce a hard, flat cookie that looked as if a monster

TABLE 4–1   Cookie Market Shares

	METROPOLITAN SÃO PAULO 1984	METROPOLITAN RIO DE JANEIRO 1984
Volume (9KG/100 Households)	669	671
Tostines	19.0	7.3
Nestlé	11.4	7.3
Monte Carlo	—	2.2
Bela Vista	1.7	0.5
Bauducco	1.4	0.2
Duchen	6.6	5.1
Petybon	3.9	0.1
Piraquê	0.7	23.8
Aymoré	—	2.0
Triunfo	4.3	6.8
Ailiram	2.7	1.8
Monstrinho Creck	—	—
Crokers	—	—
7 Boys	5.3	0.1
Marilan	2.2	2.3
Mabel	3.6	5.4
Dunga	2.0	—
Dagmel	—	4.3

Source: Audi Market— Consumer Panel

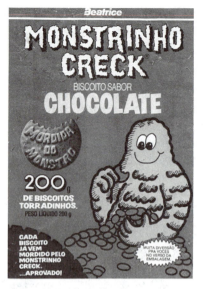

Figure 1

had taken a bite out of it. The flavors were initially chosen to be chocolate, vanilla, and coconut. (Figure 1 shows a package of the vanilla-flavored cookies.)

A whole new package design was chosen, to appeal to children between the ages of 5 and 12 years. (A survey showed that almost 50 percent of cookie consumption in Brazil is among children up to 10 years of age.) The package depicts a friendly monster taking a chomp out of a cookie on the front; on the back, some child's game is shown and a lesson about safety or other instructive message is presented. Thus, the package provides both an appealing, funny advertisement and an educational lesson.

The advertising campaign to introduce Monstrinho Creck in the São Paulo area was quite expensive. Initial estimates were for a total marketing cost of about US$500,000. As you can see from Table 4–2, the pro forma income statement for Monstrinho Creck, this expense virtually eliminates any profit for the first year of sales. But prospects for a growing profit margin and greater sales appeared very good for subsequent years. The expected return on sales of 13–15 percent was similar to that of other Beatrice products, though it does not take into account the high risk of doing business in Brazil during the debt crisis of the 1980s.

TABLE 4-2   Pro Forma Income Statement

MONSTER CHOMP (MONSTRINHO CRECK) COOKIES
3-YEAR SALES AND P + L—SÃO PAULO AND CENTER—SOUTH OF BRAZIL FORECAST

Period	MAY	JUNE	JULY	AUG	SEPT	OCT	NOV	DEC	8 Mos. 1984	%	12 Mos. 1985	%	12 Mos. 1986	%
Price Index	100							165,8	100		180		260	
Index T/Month									100		257		390	
Average T/Month									295		513		648	
Exchange rate (avrge) cruzeiros per dollar									1600/US$		2880/US$		4160/US$	
Retail Price (200 grs) (net)	600							615	—		+ 80, – %		+ 44,4%	
Ailiram S.Price (net) (200 grs) Cr$	400	423	456	484	512	545	578		—					
Ailiram S.Price (net) (1Kg) Cr$	2.000	2.115	2.280	2.420	2.560	2.725	2.890	3.075	2.551 (average)		4.592		6.631	
Ailiram Sales (tons)	120	350	280	300	330	350	330	300	2.360 Cr$ Mio		T.6.065 Cr$ Mio.		7.670 Cr$ Mio	
Net Trade Sales Cr$ Mio	240	740	638	726	845	954	954	923	6.020	100%	27.850	100%	50.860	100%
Cost									3.492	58,0	15.875	57,0	28.990	57
Gross Margin									2.528	42,0	11.975	43,0	21.870	43,0
Advertising									491	8,2	1.453	5,2	2.107	4,1
Sales Promotion Trade									122	2,0	99	0,1	—	—
" " Consumer									50	0,8	111	0,4	51	0,1
" " Merchand.									71	1,2	278	1,0	334	0,7
Market Research									49	0,8	79	0,3	51	0,1
Total Marktg. Expenditure									783	13,0	1.950	7,0	2.543	5
Gross Marktg. Contribution									1.745	29,0	10.025	36,0	19.327	38
Sales Exp.									1.264	21,0	5.292	19,0	9.663	19
Admin. Expenses									289	4,8	1.114	4,0	2.034	4
Total S&A Expense									1.553	25,8	6.406	23,0	11.697	23
Profit Contribution									192	3,2	3.619	13,0	7.630	15

P&L = profit and loss
mio = millions (of cruzeiros)
grs = grams
exp. = expenditure or expense
S&A = sales and administrative

COMPREHENSION QUESTIONS

Reading for Key Information

Answer the following questions about the case. Refer back to the reading selection if necessary.

1. Why have some companies had difficulties in selling their successful products from the home country in other national markets?

2. What problem did Pepsi-Cola encounter in Germany with its advertisement?

3. How has the food-buying pattern in Brazil changed recently?

4. How did Beatrice Companies enter the Brazilian food-processing market?

5. Describe the cookies that Ailiram produced before Beatrice assumed ownership. How does Beatrice propose to change the cookies?

6. Describe the new package design for the Monster Chomp cookies (see Figure 1).

Interpreting Financial Reports

Business Abbreviations

Refer to the pro forma income statement (Table 4–2) to see how the following abbreviations are used. What does each abbreviation stand for? Compare your answers with those of a classmate.

Cr$ _____

Exch. rate _____

P & L _____

Tot. Marktg. Exp. _____

Admin. Exp. _____

Total S&A Exp. _____

Scanning

Glance at the Cookie Market Shares Report (Table 4–1) to find the answers to the following questions.

1. What do the figures in this report represent?

2. What do the names in the left-hand column refer to?

3. The market-share information in the report comes from what two areas of Brazil? From what year?

Now scan the product launch report (Table 4–2) in order to answer these questions.

1. What is the title of the report?

2. What information does it provide?

3. What was the exchange rate for cruzeiros in U.S. dollars in 1984?

4. How much was the retail price for a 200-gram package of Monster Chomps in May 1984?

5. What percentage of profit contribution did the company forecast for the product in 1984, 1985, and 1986?

VOCABULARY DEVELOPMENT

Marketing Terms

Work on the following questions with a partner. Take turns asking each other the questions.

1. What does a *marketing manager* do?

2. Give examples of how *consumers' tastes* can be different according to age group. (Think of tastes in food, cars, music, etc.)

3. How important is *packaging* in selling a product? Give examples to support your answer.

4. What are *distribution channels?* How do they affect the sales of a product?

5. Can a company use the same *promotional strategy* in different countries? Why or why not?

Meaning from Context

Fill in the blanks with the appropriate words from the list.

advertising campaign	consumption
appealing	differentiate
chomp	displace

market survey   strategy

package design   top end

Managers of the subsidiary planned a _____ to break into the highly competitive market for sales of cookies to supermarkets. A _____ showed that about a dozen other companies already sold similar products, and Ailiram would have very little chance to _____ any of them unless it produced a _____ product.

The _____ to introduce Monstrinho Creck in São Paulo was very expensive. The cookies would sell at the _____ of the market, where only two or three other brands were competing. A new _____ was chosen that was very _____ to children between 5 and 12 years old, the ages when cookie _____ is highest in Brazil. The front of the package showed a friendly monster taking a _____ out of a cookie.

CRITICAL THINKING

Read over the questions below that are related to key issues in the case. Discuss your ideas with a partner before deciding on a response. Be prepared to explain your answers to the class.

1. How do you think it was possible for the Campbell's Soup Company, the Chevrolet division of General Motors Corporation, and Pepsi-Cola to make the expensive mistakes described in the case? How can companies avoid future errors like these?

2. Beatrice studied the market for cookies in Brazil before making its marketing plan. What did Beatrice learn about the competition, the consumer, and the popular taste for cookies in Brazil?

3. How will the Monster Chomp cookies in Brazil be different from those in the United States? Why is the company changing the cookie?

4. Why does Beatrice plan to spend a large amount on an advertising campaign for Monster Chomp cookies in São Paulo?

RESEARCH QUESTIONS

The following two questions require that you go outside of the classroom to locate English-language magazines or newspapers, as well as a magazine from your country. You may find these at a local newsstand, a library, or an American cultural center. Your teacher may suggest other possible sources.

1. Cut out an advertisement from an English-language magazine or newspaper.

   What can you learn about the company's marketing strategy from looking at the advertisement? What group of consumers does the company want to appeal to?

Photo by Christine U. Grosse

Photo by Christine U. Grosse

What does the ad tell you about the product? Does it mention price or availability?

How effective is the advertisement?

How would you change the ad to appeal to the consumers in a different country?

Be prepared to discuss your findings with a small group or the class at large.

2. Find and compare the advertisements for the same product in an English-language magazine and a magazine from your country. In what ways are the ads different? If they are identical, explain to the class why you think the company did not change the ad.

CASE ANALYSIS

As part of the marketing team for Ailiram, your job is to evaluate the newly developed strategy to market Monstrinho Creck cookies in Brazil. As you conduct your evaluation, consider the following questions: Will it be profitable for the company? Should the plan be modified in some way? You worked with Beatrice Companies in the United States on the successful Monster Chomp cookies, but this project presents a completely different challenge.

In order to make a decision, your group should consider the following points:

1. What is the marketing strategy for Monster Chomp cookies in Brazil? How does each aspect of the plan relate to the situation in Brazil?

   a. *Distribution plan*—Where will the cookies be sold? How will they by distributed?

   b. *Pricing*—Will the cookies be at the bottom, middle, or top end of the scale? Why?

   c. *Package design*—How will the package look? What are its features?

   d. *Promotional plan*—How much will the company spend on advertising? Where will it be advertised? Who are the consumers?

   e. *Product*—How does the product look? What flavors does it come in? How does it compare with the competition? Will the consumers like it?

2. In what ways does the plan take cultural differences between the United States and Brazil into consideration?

3. What is the financial outlook for the product? How profitable will it be over the next three years?

5

THE WEST AFRICAN ELECTRIC CASE

Government/business relations

Willie Alleyne Associates photograph

PREREADING EXERCISE

Discuss the following issues in class before reading the case.

1. A company that wants to invest in a foreign country usually must obtain permission from the local government. Why would a government regulate the foreign firms that want to invest in the country?

2. What conditions do governments impose on multinational firms before they are allowed to invest?

3. Does your country encourage or discourage foreign investment? For what reasons?

4. What companies manufacture electrical appliances in your country? Are they related to multinational firms?

THE WEST AFRICAN ELECTRIC CASE ======

The Current Situation

One hot afternoon in the summer of 1983, Bill Ogden was relaxing in his Lagos Holiday Inn suite. He was thinking about his efforts to negotiate the conditions for setting up a new subsidiary in Nigeria, when suddenly there was a blackout. The hotel room became thick with humidity within minutes, and the windows could not be opened. Ogden walked down the ten flights of stairs to the reception desk, where he found out that the hotel's electric generator was undergoing repairs, and power would not be restored for two hours. He decided to take a walk in the gardens of the hotel, passing under an umbrella of cool shade trees. As he walked toward the water fountain, he began to enjoy the cool breeze from the marina and started to reflect again on the status of negotiations.

He had just spent over a month in discussions with a local firm, Jaburata, Ltd., about the formation of a joint venture for manufacturing electric motors and lighting products in Nigeria. His company, Intercontinental Electric Corporation (IEC), wanted to expand its activities into sub-Saharan Africa, and the large, oil-rich economy of Nigeria appeared to be a good candidate for the first step. Subsequent careful study of the local market and competitive conditions showed that Nigeria would indeed offer excellent profit opportunities.

Just last week it had looked as though Ogden's patient efforts

This case was written by Professor Robert Grosse as a basis for class discussion. Professor Soga Ewedemi offered very helpful comments in preparing the case. 1985.

would be wasted, when the government refused to grant permission to his company for importing needed factory equipment into Nigeria. Now the situation seeded to have improved substantially, since the local partner, Babs Alotudo, had told him that a revised request to the Ministry of Industries would be approved in a few days. Ogden was not sure how Alotudo had achieved this approval, but he knew enough about the country not to be surprised.

A government representative has contended that since importation of electric motors and lighting products has a low priority for Nigeria, the importation of machinery to produce such products also should have a low priority on the list of products to be approved for import. The Nigerian government uses an import priority list to limit the outflow of foreign exchange. The country has experienced serious balance-of-payments difficulties recently as a result of the decline in the price of oil. (Oil and petroleum products account for about 90 percent of Nigeria's export earnings.) On the other hand, any industry that will use local raw materials rather than import them will be granted permission to operate in Nigeria. Since this project would use locally available raw materials where possible, Ogden's local partner was able to convince the government to permit importation of other necessary materials.

Ogden had learned from his initial inquiries that setting up an operation in Nigeria would not be easy. National law requires foreign firms to find local majority partners (to own at least 60 percent of the shares) for any direct investment in the country. Exceptions apparently have been made in the past, but Ogden found that IEC would not be permitted to retain more than 40 percent ownership of the new affiliate. Because of IEC's well-known name, several local firms expressed an interest in participating in the joint venture. The largest local electrical appliance manufacturer seemed to be the most likely candidate for partnership, but the owner of that firm was not interested in changing his current business, even for the very reasonable financial compensation offered by IEC. A second local firm with no manufacturing experience, Jaburata, Ltd., was selected, mainly because its manager, Babs Alotudo, had previously worked for Westinghouse Electric for twenty years in a variety of positions and countries. Thus, Alotudo now was involved with Ogden in seeking government approvals for ownership, financing, importing, and other contractual requirements.

Ogden had experienced some problems in dealing with the Nigerian government even with help from Alotudo. In his experience in the United States, government officials usually viewed companies as adversaries. As a result, companies there generally would pay their taxes and submit the required financial and other statements, but not request government assistance in their businesses. In

Nigeria, on the other hand, most firms seemed to receive some form of assistance from the national government in return for hiring more employees or locating in areas with less industry, or for any of several other government-selected reasons. IEC did not intend to export its motors or lighting products from Nigeria. The new affiliate would employ about 200 people and reduce current imports into the country. Based on these last two factors, there seemed to be some possibility of receiving a tax holiday (a period during which the firm pays no corporate income tax) for three years after start-up, but negotiations were still continuing.

Government bureaucrats in the Nigerian Enterprises Promotion Board (which regulates foreign investment entry) were difficult to deal with, because they often were not clear about what policy would apply to the IEC venture. Various government ministries (Commerce, Finance, Industries, and Internal Affairs) had jurisdiction over important issues such as ownership, tax incentives, profit remittances, and import licensing. Several of the issues were settled, but with the tax situation and the import license still up in the air, Ogden was frustrated. In addition, the Ministry of Finance and the Central Bank would not offer any guarantee that IEC would be able to remit its profits to the parent company in the future. He badly needed some kind of negotiating strategy for dealing with these people from a different culture whose rules were so ambiguous.

The Company

IEC is a major producer of electrical equipment in the United States. The company has been in business since 1921, and it has had overseas operations since 1932. Last year's sales were about $18 billion, in sixty-five countries. (See Table 5–1 for IEC's summary financial statements for 1982.) Though the company had been in international business for quite a while, no affiliates existed anywhere in Africa south of Egypt. The only sales in countries such as Nigeria were exports from other IEC plants, and these exports fluctuated widely from year to year as economic and political conditions changed in the African countries.

The company's main product lines are electric appliances, small and large electric motors, lighting products, and home entertainment. In each of these markets, IEC ranks between third and eighth in the United States in terms of sales volume. In overseas markets, IEC often ranks second or third behind other multinational enterprises.

IEC decided to enter the Nigerian market because its traditional markets in the United States and Western Europe were fairly saturated with both electric motors and lighting equipment. (IEC is also

TABLE 5–1   IEC Summary Financial Statements, 1982

Income Statement (in US$ millions)

Sales   17,900

BUSINESS SEGMENTS		REGIONS	
of which:		of which:	
consumer products	5,200	U.S. & Canada	13,100
industrial machinery	4,700	Europe & Middle East	2,900
electric power	3,800	Far East	1,100
nuclear power	2,400	Latin America	500
other	1,800	Africa	300
Total	17,900		17,900

Operating expenses	15,800	
wages and salaries		6,600
materials & supplies		8,800
other		400
Total		15,800
Operating margin	2,100	
Interest payments	200	
Taxes	800	
After-tax income	1,100	

Balance Sheet (as of December 31, 1982)

ASSETS		LIABILITIES & NET WORTH	
Cash	1,700	Short-term borrowing	900
Marketable securities	2,000	Accounts payable	2,100
Accounts receivable	2,900	Taxes payable	900
Inventories	2,600	Long-term debt	2,400
Property, plant, and		Shareholders' equity	7,300
equipment	4,400		
Total	13,600		13,600

diversifying into several high-tech businesses such as electronic instruments and hydroelectric power generation.) Even though IEC's products are not more advanced than those of other large companies, most of the motors and lighting equipment that would be introduced into Nigeria are now being imported, so the government is expected to welcome this import-substituting foreign investment.

The Problem

As the international division executive named to head the Nigerian operation, Bill Ogden faces both the unenviable task of negotiating to obtain acceptable conditions for IEC to enter that market, and the need to judge whether the situation is sufficiently favorable to justify investing there at all. The home-office staff recommended Nigeria as an appropriate target country, but only Ogden really knows how good or bad the local situation is. His financial manager has estimated the future cash flows of the project, and its expected net present value is positive, though not large (even without the tax holiday). Given the various risks involved, he is not certain at this point whether to go ahead with an investment. His best effort to estimate a capital budget for the proposed $U.S. 20 million project shows a positive present value under most assumptions, though the accuracy of some of his forecasts is subject to some question. If he does go ahead, he will have a factory and several hundred employees to command. If not, he probably will return to the international division staff in a medium-level position.

Ogden must now put together an overall evaluation of the terms being offered to IEC for the project, and decide on that basis whether to go ahead. So many issues are unsettled that he wants to create a bargaining strategy for concluding his dealings with the government. He wants to represent to the government how valuable the project will be to Nigeria and make a "final" request for import licenses, tax reduction, and any other permissions or subsidies that may be crucial to the project.

COMPREHENSION QUESTIONS

Answer the following questions about key facts and information contained in the case.

1. Who are Bill Ogden and Babs Alotudo?

2. Why did IEC select Jaburata, Ltd., to be its partner in the joint venture?

3. Why did the Nigerian government deny permission at first to IEC to import factory equipment into Nigeria?

4. How does Nigeria attempt to limit imports into the country?

5. What type of electrical equipment does IEC produce?

6. Why did IEC decide to enter the Nigerian market?

7. What difficulties did Bill Ogden have in dealing with Nigerian government officials?

VOCABULARY DEVELOPMENT

Paraphrasing

Restate the following sentences, substituting your own words for the underlined phrases.

1. The Nigerian government has made a priority list of products for import in order to limit the <u>outflow</u> of foreign exchange.

2. From Bill Ogden's past experience, he felt that government officials often viewed companies as <u>adversaries</u>. Companies paid their taxes and reported the required financial and other information, but did not request government assistance in their businesses.

3. The Nigerian government offered some companies <u>tax incentives</u> to invest in the country, such as a three-year period during which the firm paid no corporate income tax.

4. For many years, Intercontinental Electric Corporation's only sales in sub-Saharan Africa had been exports from other IEC plants. These exports <u>fluctuated</u> widely from year to year as economic and political conditions changed in the African countries.

Photo by Laimute Druskis

5. The home-office staff recommended Nigeria as an appropriate <u>target country</u> for investment, but only Ogden knows whether the local situation will be right for the company.

6. Ogden is concerned that so many issues remain unsettled concerning the joint venture with the Nigerian firm. He wants to create a <u>bargaining strategy</u> for concluding his dealings with the government.

Business Vocabulary

Look over the terms below to make sure that you understand their meaning. Use the glossary if you need help. Then complete the paragraph with the appropriate terms.

joint venture	raw materials	tax holiday
balance of payments	direct investment	ownership
majority partners	profit remittance	import license

Intercontinental Electric Corporation was interested in the formation of a _____ with a Nigerian firm. National law required that foreign firms find local _____ for any _____ in the country. By law, IEC was limited to 40 percent _____ of the new affiliate. Possibly the firm could receive a _____ for three years after the start-up of the company. However, the Ministry of Finance would not guarantee that it would allow _____ to the home country. Profits would have to be reinvested in Nigeria.

Since the country recently had experienced problems with its _____ , the government gave priority to any industry that would use local _____ rather than import them. For similar reasons, IEC expected to have difficulty obtaining _____ for the importation of machinery to produce electric motors and lighting equipment.

Photo by Eugene Gordon

CRITICAL THINKING

Work in small groups to discuss the following questions concerning the major issues and concepts of the case.

1. After originally denying the request, the Ministry of Industries was reconsidering IEC's request for permission to import factory equipment into Nigeria. Discuss why the Ministry may have changed its mind.

2. In what ways can Babs Alotudo be of assistance to Ogden in the negotiations?

3. How did Bill Ogden expect the Nigerian government officials to react to the joint venture? Contrast his expectations with what actually happened. Explain why the expectations and the reality were different.

4. How should Ogden approach the problem of resolving the important issues of tax incentives, profit remittances, and import licensing?

5. What cultural differences, if any, are contributing to Ogden's difficulties?

RESEARCH QUESTIONS

In order to complete this assignment, you need to conduct research outside the classroom.

1. Interview the manager of a local branch of a multinational firm or an import-export firm about the relations between the government and the company. Select the firm from the telephone directory or the list of companies supplied by the local chamber of commerce. You may conduct the interview over the telephone or in person. Prepare your questions in advance, with a partner if you prefer. Find out about:

   a. the relationship between government and business (adversarial or friendly);

   b. the regulations that government imposes on the business regarding taxes, profit remittances, ownership, and import licensing; and

   c. investment incentives to foreign firms, such as tax incentives.

   Discuss the results of the interview in class.

2. Locate an article in an English-language magazine or newspaper regarding a joint venture between a local firm and a multinational corporation. Read and summarize the article for class, focusing on its highlights.

CASE ANALYSIS

You are part of a team from Intercontinental Electric Corporation that has been assigned to assist Bill Ogden in making a decision whether to proceed with the joint venture in Nigeria. If you decide that the venture is worthwhile, you will help him plan a bargaining strategy to continue the negotiations with the government.

First you will study and evaluate the terms that the government has offered to IEC for the project, before making a decision whether to continue. Consider the following questions as you proceed with your evaluation. Add any others that you consider important.

1. What advantages does Nigeria offer as a location for a joint venture?

2. What percentage of ownership will IEC have in the joint venture?

3. What are the strengths of the partner firm, Jaburata, Ltd.?

4. What tax incentives will the firm receive?

5. Will the firm be permitted to remit profits to the home office?

6. Will the government grant the firm licenses to import needed equipment?

Decide whether IEC should go ahead with its negotiations for the project. If you think that the project is worthwhile, plan a bargaining strategy for Ogden to pursue with the government. Consider the following issues in your negotiation plan, and include any others that you think are important.

1. Value to Nigeria
2. Nigerian majority partner
3. Improved balance of payments
4. Employment opportunities
5. The company's need for import licenses, tax reductions, and other critical permissions and subsidies
6. Participation of Babs Alotudo in the bargaining

6

THE BELL SOUTH CASE

Borrowing in international financial markets

Photo courtesy of AT&T Bell Laboratories

PREREADING EXERCISE

Discuss the following questions before reading the case.

1. Who runs the telephone company in your country? Are any foreign companies allowed to compete?

2. What are some of the problems that occur when a company becomes larger and more powerful than any of its competitors?

3. What is the Eurodollar market? How can a company use it?

4. Name possible sources of funding to finance a major business project.

THE BELL SOUTH CASE

Introduction

One of the major changes in the business system of the United States in the twentieth century occurred on January 1, 1984, when the national telephone company, American Telephone & Telegraph (AT&T), was forced to sell its operating telephone subsidiaries. The U.S. Department of Justice decided to deregulate long-distance telephone service by allowing other companies to compete with AT&T. To reduce AT&T's competitive advantage over other companies, the Justice Department required that AT&T sell all of its twenty-two regional telephone operating companies (i.e., the companies that actually provided telephone service in twenty-two regions of the United States, such as Southern Bell). Now AT&T owns only a long-distance operating network of telephone service, its research division (Bell Labs), its equipment manufacturing division (Western Electric), and a new data-processing division (AT&T Information Systems).

The breakup of AT&T left the operating companies regrouped into seven corporations, with responsibility for providing local telephone service in seven areas of the United States. Such a change was truly dramatic, since AT&T had been the largest private corporation in the world. Before 1984 each operating company functioned just as a division of the national company, and each division only made decisions about telephone service in its area. Now each operating company must make *all* decisions—financing, investing, general business strategy, legal, and so on—as an independent corporation.

The decision of interest in this case is the financing decision. How should a company finance its business activities? More specifically, how should a major capital project be financed? For any large corporation, and for many medium-sized ones as well, the eurocurrency market offers very attractive financing opportunities. Bell South was chosen because its managers do not have experience in dealing with the eurocurrency markets, and it definitely should take advantage of the opportunities available there. Additional financial markets available to corporations in the United States are noted for comparison.

The Case

In the aftermath of the 1982 decision by the Justice Department, individual operating subsidiaries of AT&T were beginning to face major new decisions as soon-to-be-independent companies. Each operating company is very large by current industrial standards— Bell South alone has assets worth more than $21 billion and employs over 100,000 people. None of the operating companies has experience in large-scale financing, research and development in telecommunications, or designing a marketing strategy, since all of these functions had until now been performed by AT&T (or Bell Labs) at the national level.

One of the first priorities established by Bell South's senior management in 1983 was to initiate a research program with a laboratory facility in either Raleigh, North Carolina, or Melbourne, Florida (near major concentrations of electronics companies). Since the company would not become independent until January 1, 1984, no actual investment could take place until then. Nonetheless, Bell South's managers wanted to be ready for "independence day."

Among the more difficult problems facing Danielle Green, treasury manager for Bell South, was the issue of financing the research lab, which was estimated to cost about $25 million. Though this level of funding is not large compared to AT&T's total borrowing, it will present some difficulties for a newly independent Bell South (primarily because of this firm's inexperience at such negotiations). Ms. Green was discussing the problem with her recently hired assistant, who had just graduated from a prestigious school of business administration.

The assistant (i.e., you) proposed that they consider the idea of eurocurrency financing, through which lower interest rates are available and where there are fewer restrictions on loans. Specifically, the assistant recommended the use of a euro-deutschemark loan, which could be obtained for just over one-half of the interest cost that had been offered for a domestic, dollar-denominated loan by NCNB (North Carolina National Bank). Other alternatives had to be considered as well, of course. Table 6–1 shows various borrowing options and their costs in August 1983.

TABLE 6-1   Possible Sources of $25 Million, One-Year Borrowing for Bell South

TYPE OF FUNDING	INTEREST COST*					FEES (PAID UP-FRONT)
	US$	C$	Fr	DM	SFr	
Syndicated eurocurrency loan (LIBOR)	11.13	10.31	16.50	6.13	5.00	2.00
Eurobond issue	12.25	12.00	—	8.36	—	1.75
U.S. domestic bank loan	11.50 (prime rate)					3.00
U.S. domestic bond issue	12.65					2.25
U.S. domestic equity issue (the firm's cost of capital)	18.00					2.25
Spot exchange rate (foreign currency units/US$)	1	1.23	8.0	2.6	2.10	
1-year forward exchange rate	1	1.29	9.1	2.3	1.95	

*All interest costs are stated as annual percentage rates. If one-year loans are to be used, the rates would need to be renegotiated every year during the project. Bell South can be expected to pay a "spread" of 3/8 percent over LIBOR quotes and 1/4 percent over prime, plus the fees that are one-time, up-front charges, based on the value of the loan. Assume, for the sake of simplicity, that all interest is paid at the end of the full loan period.

LIBOR—the London Interbank Offered Rate—is the interest rate offered by banks in London for large deposits (eurocurrency deposits) from other banks. The lending rate, which varies depending on the creditworthiness of the borrower, does not have a name; it is just called "LIBOR plus the spread."

The research facility has an expected life of ten years. It will be financed each year separately, so that every year the lowest-cost source of funds should be chosen. For the first year (effective on January 1, 1984), funding will be available at the interest rates shown in Table 6-1. Each type of lender also charges fees on the loan. The fees are paid one time, at the beginning of the loan period, and they are calculated as some percentage of the total loan value (as shown). Right now, the only task is to choose the funding source for the first year; subsequent borrowing decisions will be made at the end of each year.

In addition to bank loans in the eurodollar market, Bell South can consider using a domestic bank loan. In either case, the company will pay the base interest rate plus some additional margin to the bank lender. If the company issues new bonds, it will have to pay the interest rate shown, plus the up-front fee. By issuing new stock in the company, investors would expect a return of about 18 percent per year, much higher than the bank charges. Many other financing sources exist; the choices shown are very commonly used in the U.S. market.

COMPREHENSION QUESTIONS

Locating Key Facts

Answer these questions using information from the case description.

1. What major change took place in AT&T in 1984?

2. What new functions did the operating companies assume after the breakup of AT&T?

3. Describe the size of Bell South in terms of assets and employees.

4. What was one of the priorities set by Bell South's senior management in 1983?

5. What does the term "independence day" mean within the context of the case?

VOCABULARY DEVELOPMENT

Using Prefixes to Determine Meaning

Prefixes can provide useful clues about the meaning of unfamiliar words. If you are aware of how prefixes affect the meaning of a word, you can use this knowledge to build your word-guessing power.

Look at the following words and underline their prefixes. Write the meaning of the prefix, and then the meaning of the entire word.

Photo courtesy of AT&T Bell Laboratories

After that, think of two or three other words that have the same prefix.

Underline the Prefix	Meaning of Prefix	Meaning of Word	Other Words with Same Prefix
1. aftermath	_____	_____	_____
			_____
			_____
2. dismantle	_____	_____	_____
			_____
			_____
3. deregulate	_____	_____	_____
			_____
			_____
4. telecom-munications	_____	_____	_____
			_____
			_____
5. euro-currency	_____	_____	_____
			_____
			_____
6. inexperience	_____	_____	_____
			_____
			_____

Compound Nouns as Business Terms

Many business terms consist of two nouns, where the first noun serves as an adjective to describe the second. The ability to recognize compound nouns will help you to expand your business vocabulary.

In this exercise, work with a partner to explain the meaning of the compound nouns. Think of other compound nouns with the same second noun. Then discuss with your partner how the terms relate to the Bell South case. (The first example has been done for you.)

1. marketing strategy—*plan of action used by a firm to achieve its goals to sell a product.*
   [Other compound nouns with same second verb:] *investment strategy, risk-avoidance strategy, bargaining strategy*

2. large-scale financing

3. research program

4. laboratory facility

5. electronics company

6. treasury manager

7. interest rate

Financial Terminology

The financial instruments listed here are used often in international business. Match the instrument with its characteristics. Check the glossary for definitions of unfamiliar terms.

_____ 1. U.S. domestic equity issue

a. loan from a U.S. bank

_____ 2. U.S. domestic bond issue

b. issue of stock by a company in the U.S. market

_____ 3. U.S. domestic bank loan

c. debt instrument sold worldwide by an investment bank with few restrictions

_____ 4. eurobond issue

d. loan made by a group of banks at an interest rate lower than the domestic one

_____ 5. syndicated eurocurrency loan

e. long-term debt instrument issued by a company and sold by an investment bank in the U.S. market

Business Abbreviations

The following business terms are frequently abbreviated. Working with a partner, provide the proper abbreviations.

| | |
Terms	Abbreviations
1. American Telephone and Telegraph	_____
2. research and development	_____
3. London Inter-Bank Offered Rate	_____
4. French franc	_____
5. Canadian dollar	_____
6. Deutsche mark	_____
7. Swiss franc	_____

CRITICAL THINKING

The following questions are related to key concepts presented in the case. Consider the questions carefully before responding.

1. Why did the U.S. Department of Justice force AT&T to sell its operating telephone subsidiaries?

2. Why are the financing opportunities of the eurocurrency market considered attractive by large and medium-sized corporations?

3. Describe some of the problems that the newly independent operating companies face.

4. Discuss alternative sources of funding for Bell South's US$25 million research lab.

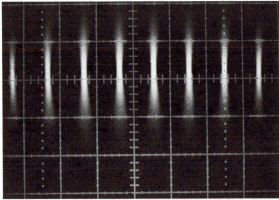

Photo courtesy of AT&T Bell Laboratories

RESEARCH QUESTIONS

This research project requires you to contact an officer of a local bank who conducts international business and collects information about the bank's interest rates and fees.

1. Contact an officer in the international section of a local bank to obtain the following information about current interest rates and fees. Find an appropriate bank from the phone directory or a list of banks doing international business from the local bankers' association or chamber of commerce. Complete the following charts with the information that you gather.

Interest Rates and Fees — one-year borrowing of US$1 million

	US$	C$	Fr	DM	SFr	Fee
Syndicated eurocurrency loan (LIBOR)						
U.S. domestic bank loan (prime rate)						

Find out the spot and forward exchange rates for the following currencies.

	US$	C$	Fr	DM	SFr
Spot exchange rate	1				
One-year forward exchange rate	1				

CASE ANALYSIS

As Ms. Green's assistant, you must weigh the possible sources of funding for the new research lab. The lab will cost US$25 million and has an expected life of ten years. Ms. Green has asked you to find answers to the following questions. Since you are new to the organization, you will work on the problem with several members of Ms. Green's staff.

Consider the following questions as you proceed with your analysis of the problem:

Question 1: What is the cheapest way to finance the research facility for the first year of operation without incurring exchange risk?

Follow these steps to solve the case. Use Table 6–1 as your source of data.

1. Which financial instrument offers the lowest interest rate for borrowing U.S. dollars? Which two instruments offer the lowest fee for initiating the loan? Now you can eliminate several of the alternatives as being too costly. Which can you eliminate?

   Choose between the two instruments, comparing interest rates and fees.

2. Of the eurocurrency loans, which one has the lowest interest rate? To eliminate exchange-rate risk, you can obtain a forward contract that guarantees the rate of exchange of dollars for the currency you borrow one year from the date of the contract.

   How much will the loan cost Bell South in interest and fees? To find out the costs, follow these steps:

   a. Borrow $25 million in Swiss francs.

   b. Convert the dollars into Swiss francs at the spot exchange rate using this formula:

   $$\text{US \$25 million} \; \frac{\text{SF}}{\substack{\text{US \$1.00} \\ \text{spot rate}}} = \text{SFr}\underline{\hspace{2cm}}$$

   c. At the end of the year, the debt is due in Swiss francs. Your forward contract guarantees the price of Swiss francs at year's end. Calculate how much Bell South will have to pay in Swiss francs at the end of the year. Remember that the interest rate is LIBOR plus the spread. Use the following formula to figure out what Bell South will owe:

   (amount of loan in Swiss francs) [1 + (LIBOR + spread)] = amount of Swiss francs to pay at year's end

d. Now convert the Swiss francs into dollars at the forward exchange rate to find how many dollars the loan will cost Bell South.

(amount of Swiss francs to be paid at end of year)

$\dfrac{\text{US \$1.00}}{\text{SF}}$ = \$_____

forward rate

cost of loan in dollars

e. In addition, Bell South must pay a fee for initiating the eurocurrency loan. How much is this fee?

7

THE HONGKONG & SHANGHAI BANKING CORPORATION CASE

Bank strategy and structure for foreign-market entry

Photo by Ray Cranbourne, used courtesy of the Hong Kong Tourist Association

PREREADING EXERCISE

Discuss the following questions:

1. Why do many banks establish branch offices in foreign countries? Which cities are famous international banking centers?

2. What are the functions of international banks?

3. Do any banks from your country have offices in the United States? What do they do there?

4. Why would a bank from HongKong want to have offices in the United States?

THE HONGKONG & SHANGHAI BANKING CORPORATION CASE

Introduction

HongKong & Shanghai Banking Corporation (HSBC) was the world's thirtieth-largest bank in 1980. Based in Hong Kong, the bank has carried out most of its business in Hong Kong dollars and U.S. dollars, with substantial amounts of business in European currencies and Japanese yen as well. It has received deposits from local (Chinese) individuals and companies, and has loaned the money to both local borrowers and international banks in the so-called eurocurrency market. HSBC has specialized in financing exports and imports, largely with firms in countries of the British Commonwealth (Great Britain and its former colonies). The vast majority of the bank's business has been done physically in Hong Kong, though it has a very large London branch office and several U.S. branches plus a subsidiary bank in California and a representative office in New York. (The representative office is not allowed to do business directly; under U.S. law it has had to refer all clients to the California subsidiary bank, the London branch, or the Hong Kong headquarters.)

In 1980 the bank was looking to expand in the U.S. market. Its dealings in the eurocurrency market had led to large deposits of U.S. dollars, British pounds, and other currencies, which the bank needed to lend to borrowers somewhere. Rather than continue to accept low

This case was written by Professor Robert Grosse as a basis for class discussion. Helpful information was provided by HSBC. Any errors of fact or interpretation are the responsibility of the author. 1986.

profits from lending these funds to other banks, HSBC decided to seek new borrowers in the world's largest market, the United States. Although HSBC had over a century of experience in international banking, it had never considered a major move into the U.S. domestic market. In the late 1970s, at a time when their British pounds, deutsche marks, and Japanese yen could buy far more dollars than in the 1950s and 1960s, many of the bank's clients were establishing offices, factories, and other investments in the United States.

The bank also was interested in moving into the U.S. market as a hedge against the substantial risk of nationalization by the Chinese government. In 1997 the British colony of Hong Kong is scheduled to return to Chinese ownership, which will bring with it the possibility of major legal changes in rules for business. Because the People's Republic of China is a communist country, many observers expect Hong Kong to lose its free market status. As the largest bank in the colony, HSBC faces very likely changes in its business activities. For this reason, the bank's managers and owners have been interested in establishing domestic activities in the United States, generally viewed as the least politically risky environment in the world.

In addition to having substantial deposits in several currencies and clients of several nationalities, the bank possessed another competitive strength—namely, its large staff of experienced bankers who knew about both lending and borrowing opportunities in Asia that were not well known to potential U.S. clients. By operating directly in the U.S. market, the bank would be able to take advantage of this expertise to earn additional profits.

HSBC has been operating in the United States since 1875, when it opened an agency in San Francisco. A second agency was opened in New York in 1880. The New York agency was converted into a branch in the 1970s, as a result of a change in New York's banking laws. In the 1960s HSBC acquired the Republic Bank of California, which had eleven branches in the state. The bank was renamed the HongKong Bank of California. Other branches were established in Chicago, Seattle, and Portland, and another subsidiary was set up in Houston. Under U.S. banking rules in 1980, if HSBC wanted to open a full-service subsidiary in any other state, then the California branch network and the Houston subsidiary would have to be divested.

The Case

Mr. Michael Sandberg, chairman of HSBC in Hong Kong, was considering the alternatives for expanding in the U.S. market in 1980. The top management of the bank wanted to diversify its assets and activities across the world, placing about one third of the total in

Hong Kong, Europe, and the United States. Sandberg felt that it would be possible to set up an agency in New York, where over 90 percent of the international banking in the United States takes place. Similarly, it would be feasible to establish a branch bank, owned completely by HSBC and using a federal U.S. charter, under the existing U.S. laws. Additional representative offices could be placed in cities other than New York, but these facilities would be restricted to providing information to potential clients, who still would need to do business with HSBC in San Francisco, London, or elsewhere outside of the United States. Finally, Sandberg considered the idea of forming a joint venture with an existing U.S. bank, which would give HSBC immediate access to new clients and partial ownership and control of the venture. Each of these alternatives is discussed in more detail below.

Setting up an *agency* would allow HSBC to minimize the capital needed to enter the U.S. market, since foreign bank agencies could use all of the capital of the parent bank as a base for their U.S. lending. The agency would allow HSBC to lend to local clients as well as Chinese or other foreign borrowers. Deposits, on the other hand, were restricted to foreign depositors—U.S. banking law forbids agencies from taking local deposits. Many foreign banks enter the U.S. market through an initial representative office, followed by expansion into an agency. While this alternative had no major financial costs, it would limit HSBC business primarily to dealing with foreign clients.

The International Banking Act of 1978 allowed foreign banks to establish *Edge Act Corporations*, subsidiaries of banks that are allowed to engage only in international banking. Edge Act Corporations may not take deposits from local residents or make loans to them for domestic business, but they may take deposits from foreign residents and lend to anyone for international business. This alternative was even more restrictive than the use of an agency, so Sandberg quickly rejected it.

A *wholly owned subsidiary*, incorporated as a normal U.S. bank, was another possibility. In this case, HSBC would need to invest enough funds in the subsidiary to start up its local lending business. Once established, the subsidiary could undertake any kind of activity allowed to domestically owned banks. This alternative would allow HSBC access to borrowing from the U.S. central bank (the Federal Reserve). The full range of borrowing and lending possibilities would be open to the new subsidiary. In order to set up a subsidiary in New York, HSBC would need to sell the California and Houston banks, since U.S. banking laws prohibited banks from owning full-service branches or subsidiaries in more than one state.

A subsidiary could be established either by creating a completely new bank with new offices and new employees, or by buying an existing bank with its existing network of offices, people, and accounts. Clearly, the second choice would be preferable, but it would cost much more. Sandberg needed to examine the expected costs of opening new offices, perhaps in New York but also possibly in San Francisco, which is closer to Hong Kong and more tied to Asian business, and where HSBC already had one subsidiary with several offices.

The use of additional *representative offices* was rejected immediately, since such offices would not allow HSBC direct participation in the U.S. market. Mr. Sandberg did realize, however, that it might be desirable to have representatives in several cities such as San Francisco, Chicago, Miami, and Los Angeles, in order to seek out additional business for the main office in New York. So representative offices were left as possibilities, to be considered only after the initial investment decision was made.

Finally, a *joint venture* with some other bank could be used. This strategy would enable HSBC to enter the U.S. market with less capital investment than the other alternatives, but it would mean sharing the decision making and the profits of the venture. A joint venture would be formed as a normal U.S. bank, similar to the subsidiary discussed above. The legal restrictions would be relatively unimportant — the key issue would be the management of the joint venture. Historically, very few joint ventures have lasted for more than a few years before the partners decided to stop the project and either operate alone or leave the market. Despite this drawback, Sandberg felt that it would be worthwhile to seek a potential partner and to compare the expected results of a joint venture with those of other alternatives.

COMPREHENSION QUESTIONS

After rereading the case description carefully, check your understanding of the case by answering these questions. Scan the case description to find the information that you need.

1. Describe the HongKong & Shanghai Banking Corporation. Include information about its size, the location of its headquarters, its clientele, and the currencies that it deals in.

2. Why does the bank want to expand into the U.S. market?

3. In what areas does the HongKong & Shanghai Banking Corporation possess expertise?

4. How long has the HSBC been in the international banking business?

5. In what city in the United States does most of the international banking business take place?

6. What are Edge Act Corporations? Where are they found?

7. What is the difference between an agency and a representative office?

VOCABULARY DEVELOPMENT

Sentence Completion

Finish the following sentences in a way that is logical and meaningful. Work with a partner on the exercise.

1. The HongKong & Shanghai Banking Corporation *is looking to expand* in the U.S. market because _____

2. HSBC can *gain access* to the U.S. market by _____

3. Mr. Sandberg was considering several *alternatives* for _____

4. The Edge Act Corporation was *rejected* as an alternative because

_____

5. One of the restrictions on operating a *representative office* in the United States is _____

6. A *wholly owned subsidiary* is a possibility that would allow HSBC to _____

Paraphrasing

Restate the following sentences, substituting your own words for the underlined words.

1. The tenth-largest bank in the world carried out most of its business in HongKong dollars.

2. The bank lent money to Chinese borrowers and international banks.

3. Since the representative office couldn't do business directly with U.S. clients, it had to <u>refer all clients to</u> the London branch or the HongKong headquarters.

4. The bank has special <u>expertise</u> in Asian <u>lending</u> and <u>borrowing</u> practices.

5. A <u>joint venture</u> with a U.S. bank would require less <u>capital investment</u> than other alternatives.

6. HSBC wants <u>to undertake</u> a new banking operation that does not have too many <u>legal restrictions</u>.

International Banking Terms

The kinds of banking operations that are permitted in a country vary from place to place, but the types of offices remain fundamen-

Photo courtesy of the HongKong Bank

tally the same everywhere. One exception is the Edge Act Corporation, which exists only in the United States.

Match the banking offices listed below with their appropriate charaacteristics, referring when necessary to the definitions provided in the case or in the glossary.

Banking Office

_____ 1. agency

_____ 2. joint venture

_____ 3. branch office

_____ 4. representative office

_____ 5. headquarters

_____ 6. wholly owned
        subsidiary

_____ 7. Edge Act Corporation

Characteristics

a. wholly owned affiliate of parent bank, not separately incorporated

b. home office, where decision makers are

c. cannot do any banking business directly, must refer business to some other affiliate of the bank

d. can use capital of parent bank as a base for U.S. lending

e. owned completely by a foreign bank, but incorporated as a regular U.S. bank

f. a subsidiary bank that may only engage in international banking

g. a partially owned subsidiary, incorporated as a regular U.S. bank

Vocabulary Building

A variety of terms are used to describe the act of starting a business in another country or closing an existing business. To become familiar with these terms, divide the following list into the appropriate categories.

to set up	to divest	to establish
to disinvest	to form	to shut down
to sell out	to go into	to buy into
to start up	to close the office	to cease operations

To Enter a Market	To Leave a Market
1.	1.
2.	2.
3.	3.
4.	4.
5.	5.
6.	6.

CRITICAL THINKING

Using the information provided in the case description, think about the following questions. Work with a partner or a small group to discuss possible approaches to the question.

1. What are some of the reasons that a foreign bank would want to set up offices in another country?

2. Discuss some of the difficulties that a foreign bank might encounter while establishing branch offices in other countries.

3. Describe the different types of offices that a foreign bank is allowed to establish abroad. Compare the advantages and disadvantages of each office.

4. If you were the manager of a foreign bank seeking to open an office in your country, where would you choose to locate the new office? Give reasons for your decision.

RESEARCH QUESTIONS

To find the answers to these questions, it will be necessary to conduct research outside the classroom.

1. Find out how many international banks operate in the city where you live. What are their names? What types of offices do they operate? (*Hint:* Look in the telephone book for the phone numbers of appropriate banks, call the chamber of commerce, or contact a local bankers' association.)

2. Select one of the international banks in your area to visit. Make an appointment with an English-speaking officer of the bank. Inter-

view her or him to discover the answers to these questions and others that you may wish to ask. Present the results of the interview to the class.

a. Where are the headquarters of the bank located?

b. What kind of office is this? What types of activities does the bank perform?

c. Does the government impose any restrictions on the bank's activities? Describe these.

d. In which currencies are most of the deposits?

e. Does the bank have other offices in the country? Where are they located? How are they different from this office?

f. Does the bank deal in the eurocurrency market? In which ways?

3. International banking is frequently in the news. Find an article in an English-language newspaper or newsmagazine about international banking. Read the article and be prepared to briefly discuss its contents with a partner or the class.

4. Discover which is the largest bank in your area in terms of deposits. Is it a domestic or an international bank?

CASE ANALYSIS

You have been appointed to a committee that is undertaking a feasibility study for the HongKong & Shanghai Banking Corporation. Mr. Michael Sandberg, chairman of the home office in Hong Kong, has asked your committee to study the possible ways that the bank might enter the U.S. market. He wants you to decide where to locate the HSBC offices in the United States, and which type of office will be the most profitable for the bank.

Mr. Sandberg has asked you to consider the following factors:

a. The new office must be profitable for the bank.

b. It should not be too costly to establish or to maintain.

c. The office should be as free as possible from government restrictions on its operations.

To analyze the case, follow these steps:

1. Decide where to locate the new office. Give reasons for your choice.

2. Decide which type of office to establish. Consider the advantages

and disadvantages of each alternative. Use the chart below to help
you choose the office that best fits Sandberg's criteria.

	Advantages	Disadvantages
1. representative office		
2. agency		
3. Edge Act Corporation		
4. wholly owned subsidiary		
5. joint venture		

3. Make your recommendations to Mr. Sandberg as to where and
   how HSBC should enter the U.S. market. Give reasons to justify
   your choices. Each committee should choose a chairperson who
   will present the recommendations to the class. After each group
   has presented its analysis, the class will decide which recommendations to follow.

8

THE FABRICA PERUANA CASE

Trade financing

Photo courtesy of the Embassy of Peru

PREREADING EXERCISE

Discuss these questions before you read the case study.

1. What products does your country import?

2. What restrictions does the government put on imported goods?

3. Why does a government restrict imports? In what ways can imports be limited?

4. If you wanted to import a product that your company needed, how would you finance the purchase?

THE FABRICA PERUANA CASE

Fabrica Peruana (FP) is a large manufacturer and importer of plastic products in Peru. The firm has specialized in the production of industrial plastics, particularly for the construction industry. Last year's sales amounted to approximately 80 billion soles. (At year-end 1984 the exchange rate between U.S. dollars and Peruvian soles was about US$1 = 5000 soles.) About 10 percent of the sales of Fabrica Peruana are exported to other countries in Latin America.

Recently, some of the firm's local clients have been requesting considerable quantities of PVC tubing (5 centimeters in diameter) for the planned construction of several apartment buildings in Lima. The tubing comes in standardized sizes and can be obtained from several North American and German suppliers. (At present, Fabrica Peruana does not produce this product.) The sales manager of Fabrica Peruana was enthusiastic about the potential new market, and he solicited information from a number of potential suppliers.

The sales manager wrote directly to the headquarters of four multinational chemical companies to obtain information about pricing and product availability. Dow Chemical Corporation, the largest producer of polyvinyl chloride (PVC) pipe in the world, declined to sell to Fabrica Peruana. Dow did not want to create competition for its own Peruvian subsidiary, which could import the tubing from Dow's U.S. factories. (Fabrica Peruana did not want to buy from the local Dow subsidiary, since that subsidiary could simply deal directly with FP's customers and take the market away from FP.) Similarly, Du Pont, BASF, and Bayer Chemical all refused to respond to FP's request for price quotations on PVC pipe.

On the other hand, a substantial number of small companies, specializing in export marketing and located in various parts of the United States, had sent letters expressing their interest in selling the

PVC pipe to Fabrica Peruana. This response occurred after FP had presented a formal request to the U.S. Embassy's Commercial Division, seeking information about U.S. exporters of plastic products. The Embassy passed the request on to the Commerce Department, which then publicized it in several bulletins to U.S. exporters. Some of the responding export firms specified that they could send sufficient quantities of tubing to meet FP's needs within one month. Without giving a precise quotation, the various exporters estimated the cost at approximately US$1.75 per meter. F.O.B. (free on board, i.e., before paying to ship the tubing to Peru).

In addition, FP's sales manager spoke directly with the export departments of Hercules Chemical Company (in Wilmington, Delaware) and Monsanto Corporation (in Cincinnati, Ohio). Hercules was very interested in the possibility of this sale, but could not send the tubing in less than eight to ten months, except for a small quantity. Monsanto had available a considerable quantity of the necessary tubing and was ready to sell to FP as soon as the deal was settled.

The terms offered by Monsanto required a minimum purchase of US$500,000 worth of the PVC pipe in six months, payable at one time. Fabric Peruana would need to obtain an irrevocable letter of credit, confirmed by Morgan Guaranty Trust Co. in New York or Miami. This agreement would allow FP to pay the full sum in 180 days. Another alternative offered by Monsanto was prepayment through a cable transfer to the account of Monsanto in Morgan Guaranty; this form of payment would enable FP to receive a discount of 10 percent in the price.

Monsanto offered to sell the 5 cm PVC tubing to FP for US$1.00 per meter, for a minimum quantity of 500,000 meters. It was expected that the cost of insurance and freight (C.I.F.) would add 15 percent to the purchase price. On top of that, the Peruvian tariff was 60 percent *ad valorem*, and additional taxes around 20 percent more *ad valorem*. (*Ad valorem* means "added on to the value"; thus, the tariff would be 60 percent of the product's cost.)

The sales manager of FP negotiated a price of US$3.50 per meter for purchases of less than 100,000 meters of the tubing and US$3.00 per meter for purchases of more than 100,000 meters with the construction companies in Lima. At the moment, it appeared certain that FP could sell 400,000 meters of the pipe, assuming that the supply from the United States were secured, since three contracts, each one for more than 100,000 meters of tubing, appeared to be virtually certain.

The sales manager thought that it would be possible to sell additional tubing to his existing clients in La Paz, Bolivia, or Santiago, Chile. The price of US$3.50 per meter was acceptable in both markets. However, the tariff in Chile was 10 percent *ad valorem*, in comparison with the 100 percent *ad valorem* tariff in Bolivia. He was not sure how these added costs to the buyers would affect their demand for the pipe. (Since the Petrochemical Sectoral Program of the Andean Pact assigned PVC tubing to Bolivia and Colombia, Peruvian firms do not receive the reduced tariff on this product. Most petrochemical products are assigned to one or more Andean Pact member countries—which include Bolivia, Colombia, Ecuador, Peru, and Venezuela—for production and tariff-free export within the group. Other member countries can only export the assigned products after paying a high tariff. Programs of this type also exist in the automotive and metalworking sectors.)

FP's financial manager was very pleased, in general, with the proposed transactions, but he was somewhat worried about the firm's creditworthiness. His normal bank, Banco Continental, did not want to offer the letter of credit needed for such a large transaction without some additional form of guarantee or collateral. From its internal working capital, FP had about one-third of the necessary funds available for the contract with Monsanto. Based on that position, the financial manager was investigating the possibility of a loan guarantee by the United States' EXIMBANK. (EXIMBANK, Export-Import Bank of the United States, is the official trade financing agency of the U.S. Government. It offers loan guarantees and subsidized loans to companies and banks in order to promote U.S. exports.) This guarantee could be used to convince Banco Continental to issue the letter of credit. He also considered the possibility of obtaining a bank loan to cover the two-thirds of the purchase price still needed.

Considering that the demand for the tubing was likely to continue in the future, the general manager judged that it was worthwhile to consider producing the PVC in the factory that FP already maintained just outside of Lima. The technology needed to produce the pipe was well known, and could be obtained through a license from any of twenty or more companies that possessed it. Two years would probably be needed to begin production, given the existing facilities and an additional investment of about US$1 million in equipment and modifications of the plant.

Thus, Fabrica Peruana faces a two-stage problem. First, the firm must decide whether or not to enter into the business of importing PVC pipe; if the answer is yes, then the firm must choose how to finance the purchase during the time before it is paid by the construction companies. Second, it must decide whether or not to begin producing PVC tubing in its own plant near Lima.

COMPREHENSION EXERCISES

Refer to the case if necessary to answer the following questions. You may work with a partner.

1. What products does Fabrica Peruana specialize in?

2. Why is the firm considering the sale of PVC pipe?

3. Why did Dow, Du Pont, BASF, and Bayer Chemical decline to quote prices for PVC to Fabrica Peruana?

4. Consider the following potential suppliers of PVC. Give reasons why Fabrica Peruana should or should not consider purchasing the pipe from them.

   a. small U.S. export firms

   b. Hercules Chemical Company

   c. Monsanto Corporation

5. Monsanto has offered Fabrica Peruana two alternatives for financing the purchase of the PVC pipe. Describe these alternatives and determine which one is better for FP.

6. Where is the potential market for Fabrica Peruana's PVC pipe?

Photo courtesy of the Export-Import Bank of the United States

VOCABULARY DEVELOPMENT

Business Terms

Explain the following terms to a partner. Refer to the case as necessary, but discuss the concepts in your own words.

1. internal working capital

2. transaction

3. letter of credit

4. collateral

5. loan guarantee

6. subsidized loan

The following business terms appear in the case study of Fabrica Peruana. Review the meaning of the terms, and then match the words with their definitions. Explain to a partner how the terms are typically used within a business context.

_____ 1. C.I.F.	a. added onto the value
_____ 2. prepayment	b. polyvinyl chloride
_____ 3. F.O.B.	c. cost of insurance and freight
_____ 4. PVC	d. ability to repay loans
_____ 5. *ad valorem*	e. without a tariff
_____ 6. creditworthiness	f. free on board
_____ 7. tariff-free	g. payment before delivery
_____ 8. EXIMBANK	h. official U.S. trade financing agency

Understanding Suffixes

A suffix is attached after the root of a word and has an effect on the word's meaning and use. An understanding of how suffixes affect words is helpful in expanding your vocabulary. Study the meaning of the following suffixes and find examples of how they are used in the case.

Photo courtesy of the Export-Import Bank of the United States

1. *-ion* is a noun suffix that means "an act, process, or condition."

   Examples from the case: *production* _____

   _____   _____   _____

   What acts or conditions do these words describe?

2. *-al* is an adjective suffix that means "related to or characterized by."

   Examples from the case: *commercial* _____

   _____   _____   _____

   What are these words related to or characterized by?

3. *-er* is a noun suffix that means "a person or a thing that is associated with something."

   Examples from the case: *manufacturer* _____

   _____   _____

   What are these words associated with?

4. *-y* is a noun suffix that means "condition, activity, or group."

   Examples from the case: *possibility* _____

   _____   _____   _____

   What condition, activity, or group is each of the words above related to?

Scanning for Figures

Glance over the case description to find the figures necessary to complete these charts.

Sales Volume for Fabrica Peruana

Sales volume of FP for last year   _____

Percentage of sales exported to
other Latin American countries   _____

Price Quotes for PVC Pipe

Cost per meter from small U.S.
companies   _____

Cost per meter for a minimum of
500,000 meters from Monsanto   _____

Percentage of *ad valorem* tariff in
Peru   _____

Percentage of *ad valorem* tariff in
Chile   _____

Percentage of *ad valorem* tariff in
Bolivia   _____

Price charged per meter by FP
on orders of less than 100,000
meters   _____

Price charged per meter by FP on
orders of more than 100,000
meters   _____

CRITICAL THINKING

Think carefully about the following questions. Discuss your ideas with a partner before deciding on your response.

1. Describe the demand for PVC pipe among Fabrica Peruana's customers.

2. What effect does the Petrochemical Sectoral Program of the Andean Pact have on the price of the tubing in Bolivia and Chile? How might this affect the demand for the product in those countries?

3. Why is Banco Continental insisting on additional guarantees from Fabrica Peruana before it issues a letter of credit for the PVC pipe transaction?

RESEARCH QUESTIONS

Contact a local company to collect information about the product it sells. You may find the company through the telephone directory or the chamber of commerce. Select a particular product that is produced or sold locally, such as PVC pipe, and find out the following facts. Report your findings to the class.

1. Obtain pricing and product-availability information about the product from a local company. Find out the cost of the product for varying quantities. Is there a discount for prepayment?

2. Inquire about the availability of the product. How soon can the

Photo by Christine U. Grosse

company deliver a certain quantity of the product? Are there any restrictions on its availability?

3. What are the export and import tariffs attached to the product, if it is sold abroad or imported from abroad?

CASE ANALYSIS

The general manager of Fabrica Peruana has asked for your committee's advice on several important decisions that he must make. Consider the following issues as you think about what advice you will give him.

1. Should Fabrica Peruana enter into the business of importing PVC pipe?

   To make this decision, you must decide whether the business is profitable or not.

a. Consider which supplier the company should use.

b. Calculate how much Fabrica Peruana will pay for the PVC pipe, and how much the company will earn by selling the pipe to its customers.

c. Subtract the earnings from the cost to determine how much profit the company will make. (*Hint:* You should calculate profitability for different amounts of pipe that might be sold to different customers.)

2. If the answer to question 1 is yes, how can the company finance the purchase of PVC for the period before it receives payment from its customers?

3. Decide whether Fabrica Peruana should begin production of PVC tubing.

a. Do you think the market for PVC will decline, continue steady, or grow in the future?

b. Should this decision be made now or later? Why?

9

THE U.S. AUTO INDUSTRY CASE

Competitiveness between countries

Photo courtesy of the General Motors Corporation

PREREADING EXERCISE

Discuss the following questions:

1. Name the world's most important automobile companies.

2. In your opinion, what company makes the most reliable cars? Which makes the most beautiful cars?

3. What is the reputation of Japanese cars in your country? Of American cars?

4. What factors influence the price of a car?

THE U.S. AUTO INDUSTRY CASE

The U.S. domestic auto industry has suffered a dramatic decline in output, employment, and market share during the past decade. In 1973 total U.S. production was 9.4 million cars per year, total employment was about 1.1 million workers, and the market share of domestic companies was about 85 percent. By 1982 these levels had fallen to 6 million cars per year, 740,000 workers, and a 71 percent market share, as depicted in Figure 9–1.

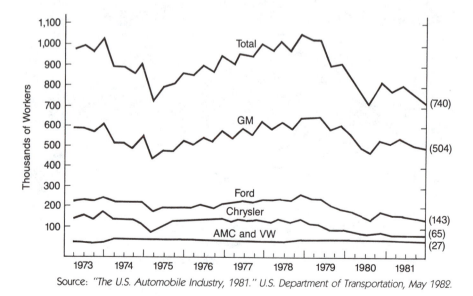

Source: "The U.S. Automobile Industry, 1981." U.S. Department of Transportation, May 1982.

FIGURE 9-1   Employment by U.S. Auto Manufacturers since 1973.

These discouraging statistics for one of America's showcase industries dramatize the serious competitive problems also faced by U.S. steel, chemicals, appliances, and other manufacturing sectors in international competition.

The decline in the automotive industry began with the oil crisis of 1973–74, when gasoline prices rose over 300 percent. Almost immediately, consumers began switching to smaller, more fuel-efficient cars—which are the strengths of the major auto importers (Volkswagen, Nissan, and Toyota). This shift in demand from large to smaller cars did not reverse itself later in the 1970s, and the foreign importers continued to gain market share. Detroit's efforts to produce competitive small cars were limited by its continuing expectation that large-car demand would soon resume. So only slowly did the domestic industry put its resources into small-car production, resulting in inadequate domestic supply as well as inadequate concern for "value"—that is, quality and performance relative to price. During this period, consumers discovered that similarly priced imports generally offered better performance and fewer problems than U.S. -produced cars, and this factor too has continued to haunt GM, Ford, and Chrysler.

Crisis conditions continued into 1984, even as the Big Three began to show renewed profitability in the current business-cycle upswing. Production costs and auto "quality" remained substantially worse for U.S. manufacturers than for the Japanese, notwithstanding U.S. advertising campaigns ("Quality Is Job 1," "If you can find a better car, buy it," "GM, Mark of Excellence"). Though the firms reenter the fray much leaner and more responsive to foreign competitors, the evidence still does not paint an optimistic picture as is apparent from the consumer opinions shown in Table 9–1.

Consider first the cost conditions facing the eight largest competitors in the U.S. market. Table 9–2 presents several comparisons, starting with raw production data, then adjusting for the degree of vertical integration of the firms and for the differences in average size of car produced.

According to a study by Abernathy, Harbour, and Henn ("Productivity and Comparative Cost Advantages: Some Estimates for Major Automotive Producers," Feb. 13, 1981), fully adjusted costs show a Japanese advantage over U.S. producers of about $1200–$2200 per car. Even GM, the most cost-efficient U.S. producer, averages close to $900 more per car than the least cost-efficient Japanese producer, Toyota.

Table 9–3 shows more details concerning various input costs, which together lead to an overall average cost differential of $1650 per car, again favoring the Japanese.

TABLE 9–1 Quality Comparisons of Foreign and Domestic Automobiles—1979

AUTOMOTIVE CLASS	CONDITION OF CAR AT DELIVERY (Scale of 1-10, 10 Is Excellent)				OWNER SATISFACTION (Percentage That Would Buy Again)			
	Total	Domestic Make	Domestic Captive	Imports	Total	Domestic Make	Domestic Captive	Import
Subcompacts	7.15	6.55	7.15	7.94	82.9	76.6	83.9	91.0
Lightweight						83.0	—	—
Heavier						71.0		
Small specialties	6.55	6.33	7.02	7.80	79.9	77.6	85.6	92.5
Compacts	6.30	6.20	—	7.65	72.4	72.2* 77.4**	—	91.4
Mid-size	6.63	6.51	—	8.05	76.9	75.3	—	94.5
Standard	6.75	6.75	—	—	81.8	81.8	—	—
Luxury	7.21	7.12	—	8.47	87.2	86.6	—	94.6

*Low-price domestic compacts

**High-price domestic compacts

Source: Rogers National Research, Buyer Profiles, 1979 (data aggregated from proprietary data). From "The U.S. Automobile Industry, 1980," U.S. Department of Transportation.

TABLE 9-2   Calculation of Unit Costs

(A) Taken from corporate reports:

	MATERIALS	LABOR	CAPITAL	S&A	TARIFF	TOTAL
American Motors	$4246	1891	150	658	—	36945
Chrysler	5699	2812	284	425	—	9220
Ford	5181	2565	306	324	—	8376
General Motors	3725	3174	389	302	—	7590
Nissan	2619	450	286	880	400	4636
Toyo Kogyo	2252	566	260	566	400	4044
Toyota	3394	407	261	232	400	4694
Volkswagen	6009	2252	358	418	400	9437

(B) Adjusted for 50 percent vertical integration:

American Motors	3540	2545	202	658	—	6945
Chrysler	4262	4108	415	425	—	9210
Ford	4120	3514	419	324	—	8377
General Motors	4055	2881	353	302	—	7591
Nissan	2202	704	448	880	400	4634
Toyo Kogyo	1954	851	407	566	400	4178
Toyota	2275	1080	693	232	400	4679
Volkswagen	4581	3483	553	418	400	9435

(C) Adjusted to reflect comparable product mix:

American Motors	2833	2290	202	658	—	5983
Chrysler	2557	3492	415	425	—	6889
Ford	2472	2987	419	324	—	6202
General Motors	2433	2449	353	302	—	5537
Nissan	2202	704	448	880	400	4634
Toyo Kogyo	1954	851	407	566	400	4180
Toyota	2275	1080	693	232	400	4679
Volkswagen	4581	3483	553	418	400	9435

Source: William Abernathy, James Harbour, and Jay Henn, "Productivity and Comparative Cost Advantages: Some Estimates for Major Automotive Producers," Harvard Business School Working Paper, February 13, 1981.

Notice that the single most important factor in Japanese competitiveness is *not* government subsidies or a policy of "dumping" cars in the U.S. market; rather, it is labor cost. This difference of almost $2000 per car favors the Japanese producers so strongly that all other comparisons virtually can be ignored.

Labor cost can be viewed from two distinct perspectives. First, wage rates can be compared directly, ignoring differences in output per worker. Table 9-4 compares wages in eight of the major manufacturers that sell in the United States. As described in Table 9-3, this difference in wage costs alone accounts for about one-half of the

TABLE 9–3 Total Cost Advantage, 1979

A Cost Summary and a Comparative Reconciliation of Two Analytical Approaches

	ANALYSIS A—BASED ON AGGREGATE FINANCIAL AND OTHER DATA			ANALYSIS B— BASED ON HARBOUR & ASSOC. LABOR DATA
	U.S., per vehicle	Japanese, per vehicle	Japanese advantage	
Materials	$ 2575	$ 2145	$ 430	430ᵇ
Labor cost	2800	880	1,920ᵈ	612
Japan wage difference				564ᵇ
Capital charges	350	515	(135)	325
Warranty cost				95
Selling and administrative	425	560	(165)	(165)ᵇ
Transportation and tariff	0	400	(400)	(400)ᵇ
Landed cost advantage	$ 6150	$ 4500	$ 1,650	$1,461.0

ᵇNot considered in the Harbour & Assoc. analysis but added from the U.S. Department of Transportation's analysis of financial data to offer comparable total cost comparisons.

ᵈ$955 attributable to wage rates.
 $965 attributable to productivity.

Source: Abernathy, Harbour, and Henn, "Productivity and Comparative Cost Advantages."

TABLE 9–4 Estimated Total Labor and Fringe Compensation, Hourly and Total, for Selected Automotive Manufacturers (1979)

FIRM	HOURLY	TOTAL
American Motors	$15.60	$17.25
Chrysler	16.49	19.91
Ford	15.94	20.92
General Motors	15.25	19.15
Nissan	—	9.59
Toyo Kogyo	—	11.00
Toyota	9.63	11.99
Volkswagen (Europe)	16.77	—

Source: Abernathy, Harbour, and Henn, "Productivity and Comparative Cost Advantages."

total cost difference. The gap had narrowed from 1975, when Japanese auto workers received compensation at a rate that equaled only 37 percent of the wages paid in the U.S. industry. Devaluation of the yen since 1979 has essentially halted the trend toward equalizing wage costs for the moment.

The second aspect of labor cost is productivity. Even if wages were equal in both countries, the output of Japanese workers has been consistently much higher than that in the United States. Table 9–3 attributed about half of the total cost difference to this factor; Table 9–5 disaggregates the productivity measure into specific components.

Together, wage costs and productivity give Japanese firms approximately a 40 percent cost advantage over U.S. firms. It is not possible to place all of the difference on the shoulders of the United

TABLE 9–5   Summary of Japanese Productivity Advantage (at $16/hour U.S. wage)

		PER VEHICLE	
		Hours	Cost
Technology/stamping	Manpower	4.3	$ 69
	Depreciation	—	35
Management systems/techniques			
Just-in-time production	Manpower	2.5	40
	Scrap	—	45
	Interest cost	—	90
Quality-control systems	Manpower	6.5	104
	Warranty		95
Other manufacturing productivity (Quality circles programs)	Manpower	10.2	163
Plant sizes/complexes/ locations	Manpower	4.1	66
	Other mfg. costs		35
	Inbound freight		120
Material handling engineer	Manpower	0.8	13
Union-management relations/ negotiations			
Relief allowances/practices	Manpower	3.0	48
Absentee	Manpower	0.7	12
	Fringes		39
Union representatives	Manpower	0.6	10
Japanese-purchased services and staff functions		3.0	48
Total Japanese advantage	Manpower	35.7	$612
	All other	—	420
Less purchased services/staff		3.0	(48)
Net Japanese productivity advantage		32.7	$984
Summarized subcategories:			
Manpower			$564
Capital charges, supplies, and scrap			325
Write-off, warranty			95
Total			$984

Source: Harbour & Associates

Auto Workers, since the productivity disadvantage stems substantially from factors controlled by management (e.g., inventory policy, quality control systems, and plant size and location). Each of these factors has been studied carefully by General Motors, Chrysler, and Ford, but the changes that they have made have not yet reduced the gap substantially.

Every U.S. auto manufacturer has taken heed of the Japanese challenge. All of them use "quality circles" or some analogous form of worker participation in shop floor decisions. Quality circles are small teams of workers and supervisors who meet regularly to discuss working conditions and suggestions for improvement in product quality and productivity. The circles give workers more active participation in decision making in the company. The "just-in-time" inventory policy also has been implemented widely in the domestic industry and has cut inventories significantly. "Just-in-time" signifies that inventories are kept at very low levels, and inputs are ordered so that they arrive just in time for use. Plants are being renovated or relocated, as well as discontinued where necessary. All of these steps represent a positive and determined reaction to the challenge. Still, there remains (in 1984) a substantial Japanese cost advantage.

COMPREHENSION QUESTIONS

Scanning for Factual Information

Scan the case description for the information necessary to answer the following questions.

1. What factors give the Japanese a substantial cost advantage over U.S. auto manufacturers?

2. What percentage of its market share has the U.S. auto industry lost over the past decade? Why has its market share declined?

3. What trend has employment in the U.S. car industry followed during the past ten years? How can you explain this trend?

4. Why did American consumers switch to smaller, more economical cars in the 1970s? How did the U.S. car manufacturers respond to this movement?

5. Describe the U.S. automobile industry's ad campaigns.

Interpreting Charts and Graphs

Charts and graphs are often used in business reports and pre-sentations to summarize important information in a clear, concise format. Businessmen and -women need to know how to read charts and graphs with ease and how to extract information and draw con-clusions from them.

Six graphs and charts appear in this case study. The following exercises provide practice in reading and interpreting the information in each graph and chart.

Figure 9–1

Understanding the Graph

1. What is the title of this graph?

2. What do the numbers along the left margin (*y* axis) of the graph indicate?

3. What do the numbers in parentheses on the right side indicate?

4. What years does the graph cover?

5. Which auto manufacturers are represented in the graph?

Interpreting the Information

1. When did employment figures reach their lowest point? Their highest point? What do these high and low points reflect?

2. What was the trend in employment from 1979 through 1981?

3. Which company employs the most people?

4. Have all the U.S. car producers experienced the same trends in employment? Give a possible explanation for your answer.

Table 9–1

Understanding the Chart

1. What is the title of the chart?

2. What scale is used in the chart?

3. How is owner satisfaction measured in the chart?

4. Where are the "domestic" cars made? Where do the "imports" come from?

Interpreting the Chart

1. When domestic-make cars are compared with imports with respect to condition of the car at delivery, how do the compacts fare? How do all classes compare?

2. Whose opinions are recorded in this chart?

3. With regard to owner satisfaction, how do imports compare to domestic-make cars in mid-size models? In all models?

4. What does this chart say about consumer perceptions of quality in domestic and imported cars?

Table 9–2

Understanding the Chart

1. What is the title of the chart?

2. What does "unit cost" refer to?

3. S&A means "selling and administrative." Which auto producer has the highest S&A cost?

4. Which categories are adjusted for vertical integration?

Interpreting the Information

1. Which company pays the most for materials?

2. Which three companies have the highest labor costs?

3. Why do some companies have to pay a tariff?

4. Which three companies have the lowest total unit cost?

Table 9–3

Understanding the Chart and Interpreting the Information

1. What is the title of the chart?

2. Compare the U.S. and Japanese labor cost per vehicle.

3. Compare the U.S. and Japanese materials cost per vehicle.

4. How much is the total Japanese cost advantage?

Table 9–4

Understanding the Chart and Interpreting the Information

1. What does this chart show?

2. What is fringe compensation?

3. Which company pays the lowest hourly wage (including fringes)?

4. Which company pays the highest hourly wage (including fringes)?

5. How do wages paid by the American car companies compare with those paid by Japanese firms?

Table 9–5

Understanding the Chart and Interpreting the Information

1. What is the title of the chart?

2. The cost of manpower per hour is calculated at $16 an hour, the U.S. wage. Why is this?

3. What is the net Japanese productivity advantage in terms of dollars?

4. In what areas do the Japanese have a productivity advantage over the American car manufacturers?

VOCABULARY DEVELOPMENT

Paraphrasing

Restate the following sentences, substituting your own words for the underlined word or expression.

1. Since 1982 there has been a 20 percent devaluation of the yen.

2. U.S. auto manufacturers have taken heed of the Japanese challenge.

3. All of the U.S. auto companies use some form of quality circles in making shop floor decisions.

4. The just-in-time inventory policy has cut inventories significantly.

5. Productivity can be disaggregated into specific components such as management systems, quality-control systems, and so on.

Photo courtesy of the General Motors Corporation

Sentence Completion

Choose the appropriate ending to the following sentences:

1. The *Big Three* American car manufacturers are

   a. Mercedes Benz, Rolls Royce, and BMW.

   b. Toyota, Volkswagen, and Datsun.

   c. Ford, Chrysler, and General Motors.

2. *Business cycle* refers to

   a. a repeating series of booms and recessions in an economy.

   b. internal problems that businesses must face.

   c. external factors that affect company productivity.

3. An *ad campaign* helps a company to

   a. cut production costs.

   b. promote its products.

   c. improve the quality of its products.

4. When firms *reenter a fray much leaner*, they

   a. go into competition with reduced expenditures.

   b. go into a recessionary period.

   c. go into bankruptcy.

5. Companies that have a high degree of *vertical integration* are those which

   a. own other companies that produce most of the components or raw materials used in the manufacturing process.

   b. have invested in factories outside of their national boundaries.

   c. have entered into partnerships with competitors.

6. Japan has been accused of *dumping* cars on the U.S. market—in other words,

   a. selling cars at unfairly low prices to penetrate the market.

   b. selling more cars than legally allowed.

   c. selling defective cars.

7. If a carmaker is relatively *cost-efficient*, it

   a. has relatively low production costs.

   b. produces higher-quality automobiles.

   c. pays union wages to all employees.

8. *Input costs* for automobile manufacturers consist of

   a. materials and labor cost.

   b. the interest rates on company loans.

   c. revenues minus expenditures.

Business Terms

Many business terms refer to increases or decreases in currency values, interest rates, profits, prices, expenditures, and so on. Put each of the following words into the appropriate category.

boost	shoot up	rise	drop
collapse	double	triple	step up
go down	fall	jump	boom
bust	decline	wane	slacken

Increase	Decrease
1.	1.
2.	2.
3.	3.
4.	4.
5.	5.

Increase	Decrease
6.	6.
7.	7.
8.	8.

CRITICAL THINKING

Think about the questions below. Compare your ideas with those of a partner. Be prepared to discuss your answers in class.

1. What changes have occurred in the U.S. auto industry in the past decade? What caused these changes?

2. Why are Japanese auto producers more cost-efficient than American car manufacturers?

3. What is the most important single factor in Japanese competitiveness?

4. Compare the cost of labor in Japan and the United States. What two aspects make up the cost of labor?

5. How have the U.S. auto manufacturers responded to the Japanese challenge?

6. What else should the U.S. automakers do to compete more effectively with the Japanese?

RESEARCH QUESTIONS

To complete this assignment, it is necessary to contact two automobile dealerships in person or by telephone. You will speak to a salesperson at an American and a Japanese car dealership in order to find out the following information, and any additional information that you choose. Compare your findings from the two competitors and present the results in class.

1. What is the lowest-priced model on the lot? What features does it have?

2. Obtain a breakdown of the costs of a particular car. Compare the costs to those of a similarly priced car at the competitor's lot. How do the costs of individual items (such as air-conditioning, AM/FM radio, power steering, tinted windshield, shipping) differ?

Photo courtesy of the General Motors Corporation

3. Ask the dealer how the car compares to a similarly priced model on the competitor's lot in terms of quality, performance, style, and features.

4. Is the sales price negotiable? What terms are available for financing the car?

CASE ANALYSIS

You have just been hired as a member of a consulting team to one of the Big Three auto manufacturers in the United States. Your assignment is to formulate a series of recommendations for the company's board of directors, advising them how to avert financial disaster and return to profitability.

Work in a group of three to five people. Reread the case description and look over the charts and graphs as you consider the key issues below. Identify the most serious problem(s) confronting the auto industry and make recommendations on how to solve them. Support your recommendations with the facts from the case.

Your report to the board of directors should include the following information:

1. Statement of the problem—Why has the U.S. auto industry declined?

2. Method of analyzing the problem—What are the competitive disadvantages (and advantages) of the firm?

U.S. auto makers are relatively less competitive than the Japanese on the bases of (see Tables 9–2, 9–3,and 9–4):

a. labor costs

b.

c.

d.

e.

U.S. auto makers are relatively more competitive on the bases of:

a. delivery costs (transportation plus tariff)

b.

c.

d.

3. Analysis of the problem—Which of the preceding issues are most important? Support your choices with facts from the case.

4. Recommendations to the company—Which of these strategies will be most helpful to your company? Give reasons for your choices, and tell how the strategies can improve the condition of the firm. Finally, describe ways in which the company can carry out the plans.

Strategies for the U.S. auto manufacturer

1. Cut labor costs.
2. Increase productivity.
3. Raise fuel efficiency.
4. Improve perception of quality (warranties, etc.).
5. Seek U.S. government help.
6. Move plants to Japan.

10

THE IBM CONSUMER ELECTRONICS CASE

Logistics

Photo courtesy of IBM

PREREADING EXERCISE

Discuss the following questions:

1. Logistics involves the transportation of materials to a factory and the shipment of goods to the market. In what ways is logistics important to the success or failure of a company?

2. What products does IBM make? Who are its typical customers?

3. Which companies make personal computers? Which has the largest market share?

4. Describe the market for personal computers. Who buys them? For what reasons? What is the price range for PCs? Have sales increased or decreased recently? Why?

THE IBM CONSUMER ELECTRONICS CASE ══════

Introduction

One aspect of business administration that often is ignored by managers seeking to increase their revenues or decrease their production costs is *logistics*. Logistics is the process of bringing together production inputs for manufacture. It also involves the process of physically transporting the firm's products to customers. (Another term often used in the same sense as *logistics* is *transportation management*.) This part of a company's business may play an important role in the success (or failure) of any project.

The main goals of logistics management are (1) to minimize the costs of transporting inputs and products, and (2) to minimize the risks involved in this process. In today's MBA (Master of Business Administration) programs, students receive specific training in techniques for minimizing logistics costs, generally through the use of *linear programming models*. These models attempt to measure every possible alternative for transporting the materials, and then select the one that costs the least. An example is given below. While linear programming models do not generally include risk as a measurable factor, they can be adapted to do so. (Although risk considerations should be included, to avoid complexity they are not presented here.)

This case was written by Professor Robert Grosse as a basis for class discussion. All numerical information was created by the author to illustrate the kind of logistical problem facing IBM at the time.

COSTS	LOCATION	
	A	B
Sale price per unit	$1.00	$1.25
Total production cost per unit	.50	.60
Transportation cost to		
market A or B	.40	.20

To illustrate the linear programming model, assume that XYZ Incorporated wants to ship its products to customers in two locations, A and B. Costs of production and transportation are shown in the preceding table.

In this example, even though production costs are lower in location A, the company will be better off producing in location B and serving both locations from there. The total delivered cost from location A is $0.90 per unit, while from B it is $0.80 per unit.

The example would become more complex if the production capacity were limited in each location, so that some production were necessary in both places to fully serve the market. More detailed estimates of costs (to include both fixed and variable costs) also would add to the difficulty of choosing an alternative. Nonetheless, such logistics problems can be solved in the same general way that was used here. (Risk could even be included as a factor. The company could choose to produce some products in each location, so that problems in either one would not shut shown the firm completely.) The situation facing IBM Corporation in the early 1980s requires exactly such a solution.

The Case

The International Business Machines Corporation (IBM) had been suffering a protracted decline in market share, though not in sales or profits, during the decade of the 1970s. This situation was virtually unknown in the history of the company since the 1940s. Part of the problem lay in organizational inertia; the firm had grown to a size at which its annual sales amounted to billions of dollars without experiencing any single internal crisis. Another part was the antitrust suit brought by the U.S. Justice Department in 1968, which continued into the early 1980s, sapping corporate resources constantly.

In the late 1970s, IBM Chairman Frank Cary took the bold step of moving the company into consumer electronics, and away from its traditional focus on industrial and government markets. This step required an effort of about five years and several billion dollars of investment before any marketable products resulted. In late 1981, IBM introduced its Personal Computer (PC), a tabletop computer which sold for less than $5000. This machine had the capacity to carry out distributed data processing, and could also function as a remote terminal for a mainframe computer. The main initial functions intended for the PC were word-processing (in which the PC competes directly with IBM's own Datamaster word processor) and data manipulation, such as bookkeeping and other simple financial tasks.

Initially, the PC was assembled entirely in IBM's new plant in Boca Raton, Florida. After only a few months of operation, demand began to outstrip production at this plant. Even a substantial expansion in 1981 was inadequate to meet the growing market needs. It became clear that demand for the machine would far exceed IBM's projections, and the search began for additional production capacity.

The choices for additional PC production (and also production of the second version of the personal computer, called the XT) were narrowed down to Boca Raton, Scotland, and the Texas-Mexico border region. These locations were selected on the basis of production costs, access to markets, and ease of operation in conjunction with the existing Boca Raton facility. Table 10–1 presents some of the considerations involved in IBM's decision.

TABLE 10–1 Pro Forma Costs of New PC Production (per unit)*

| | Location | | |
ITEM	BOCA RATON	SCOTLAND	MEXICO
Components and other inputs	$290	$300	$350
Assembly	150	100	50
Transportation to market	50	80	100
Administrative costs	10	30	60
Tariff costs	0	100	0
Annual fixed costs	$30.5 million	$25.1 million	$17.3 million

*All costs are shown in U.S.$ per unit, with a minimum scale of 1,000,000 units per year of production (except fixed costs). These data were created by the author and do not necessarily relate to IBM's actual costs.

In mid-1983 IBM's senior management was grappling with the difficult question of locating this new facility. Production capacity would be approximately 2 million personal computers per year, which was anticipated to be approximately half the total demand. The rest would be produced by the existing facility in Boca Raton. The only consumer market considered was the United States; shipments to other countries were expected to be small for a few years.

COMPREHENSION QUESTIONS

Reading for Factual Information

Answer the following questions, referring to the case description if necessary.

1. Describe the two main goals of logistics management.

2. What is a linear programming model? How is it used in transportation management?

3. What did IBM lose gradually over the decade of the 1970s? Discuss the reasons for this decline.

4. How did IBM Chairman Frank Cary dramatically redirect the focus of the company?

5. What new IBM product appeared in 1981? How much did it cost?

6. Where did IBM assemble the PC? What problem occurred shortly after production began?

Interpreting Tables

Look at Table 10−1 to find the answers to the following questions.

1. What is the title of Table 10−1? What information does it contain?

2. Which locations are compared in the table? Which costs are included?

3. How much is the per-unit cost of transportation to the market for PCs that are produced in Scotland? In Mexico? In Boca Raton? Which location has the cheapest transportation cost?

4. Compare the costs of the components and other inputs at each of the three locations. Which is the least expensive?

5. How much more does it cost to assemble the PC in Boca Raton than in Mexico? Why do you think assembly is more expensive in Florida?

6. What is the minimum scale of units per year of production?

Photo courtesy of IBM

VOCABULARY DEVELOPMENT

Paraphrasing

Restate the following sentences, substituting your own words for the underlined phrases.

1. Logistics is one aspect of business administration that can help managers to increase their revenues.

2. The primary goal of transportation management is to minimize the costs of transporting inputs for manufacture and finished products.

3. Logistics plays an important role in the financial success of a company.

4. Production costs are lower in certain locations as a result of labor and raw materials.

5. A strike by company employees shut down the factory and created an internal crisis for the firm.

6. The annual fixed costs for the company exceeded $30 million.

Nouns and Verbs

Many business terms have the same form whether they function as nouns or verbs. The list below consists of such words. Working with a partner, use each term first as a noun and then as a verb in sentences of your own.

1. market

    (*noun*) _____

    (*verb*) _____

2. cost

    (*noun*) _____

    (*verb*) _____

3. process

    (*noun*) _____

    (*verb*) _____

4. risk

    (*noun*) _____

    (*verb*) _____

5. estimate

    (*noun*) _____

    (*verb*) _____

6. decline

    (*noun*) _____

    (*verb*) _____

7. profit

    (*noun*) _____

    (*verb*) _____

In other cases, the noun and verb forms of business terms are closely related. Simply by adding a -*tion* suffix to the verb's root, you can create the noun form. Give the noun or verb form of each word in the exercise that follows.

Verb	Noun
1. produce	_____
2. _____	transportation
3. anticipate	_____
4. _____	expectation
5. locate	_____
6. _____	introduction
7. administer	_____
8. _____	situation
9. consider	_____
10. _____	operation

CRITICAL THINKING

Respond to the following questions after exchanging ideas with a partner.

1. In the linear programming model shown in the case, why should the company produce in location B instead of location A?

2. Why might companies choose to produce some products in a variety of locations, instead of all in one location?

3. On what basis did IBM select Boca Raton, Scotland, and Mexico as possible sites for PC production? Discuss the advantages and disadvantages of each site.

4. How should IBM select the best site for the PC plant? Which factors are the most important in making this decision?

RESEARCH QUESTIONS

These two research projects involve searching for information outside of the classroom. The local chamber of commerce will help you identify a firm for the first project, and you may find a relevant article in an English-language magazine or newspaper at a newstand or library in your area.

1. Which international firms have recently opened an office in your area? Select one of the firms and contact the general manager in

Photo courtesy of IBM

order to discover the company's reasons for locating in the region. Some possible reasons might be:

1. tax incentives
2. access to market
3. access to labor force
4. access to manufacturing inputs
5. government incentives to foreign investment
6. good climate
7. personal reasons

2. Find an article in an English-language newspaper or magazine concerning IBM or personal computers. Read the article and prepare a three-to-five-minute oral summary of the major points treated in the article.

CASE ANALYSIS

The senior management of IBM has asked for your advisory group's assistance in deciding where to locate the new manufacturing facility for the Personal Computer. Consider the following key issues before making your recommendatons.

1. *The present and future market for PCs* (current version and XT).

2. *Production capacity and demand.* (Consider the capacity of the present facility as well as the new facility.)

3. *Access to markets.*

4. *Production costs.* (In calculating the production costs, consult Table 10–1. Compare the costs per unit at each of the three locations. Remember to multiply each total by the number of units of production per year. Then add the annual fixed costs for the three locations.)

Make your report to the senior management, stating which site should be chosen and why.

11

THE PRODUCTOS DE MADERA CASE

Capital budgeting

Photo courtesy of M. Silver Associates, Inc.

PREREADING EXERCISE

Discuss these questions in class before reading the case.

1. How would you decide whether or not to build a motorcycle plant in the United States if you worked for Honda Motors?

2. What does *cash flow* mean? How does cash flow affect the success of a business? How does it relate to the decision for Honda in question 1?

3. If you wanted to set up a sales office in England, would you prefer to have your sales in British pounds or in your own currency (for example, Indian rupees)? Why?

4. How does a company decide what price to charge for a product?

THE PRODUCTOS DE MADERA CASE

Introduction

To operate a business successfully, the manager needs to make decisions that maximize the returns to the owners of the company. Such decisions range from buying supplies from high-quality, low-cost suppliers, to hiring the best available workers, to investing in the best available projects. This case focuses on the problem of evaluating potential projects for investment—that is, the *capital budgeting decision*.

The usual object of capital budgeting analysis is to measure the expected cash flows that will result from potential investment projects, and to choose which projects to undertake. The most important factors to be measured are the amount of money needed for the original investment, the cost of obtaining those funds, and the future revenues and costs that the project will generate. The appropriate measure of these cash flows is the present discounted value of each of them (i.e., what each flow would be worth today, even though it will occur at some time in the future). To simplify our analysis, let us just look at the cash flows involved in the present project and try to judge on that basis whether it is a worthwhile project.

Any investment project in another country is complicated by the fact that more than one currency is involved (American dollars and Costa Rican colones in the present case). It is often difficult to judge the impact of a change in the exchange rate on future cash flows. The data in this case are based on estimates of the future exchange rate.

The Productos de Madera case involves a fairly large company in Costa Rica that is trying to find a strategy to escape the deep economic recession that has existed for several years. One possibility is to enter the U.S. market. This is the project that must be evaluated.

The Case

Sr. Jorge Michelson was sitting in his San José office early one morning in mid-1984, thinking about the difficulties that he faced in importing parts (fittings) for the wooden stereo cabinets and other furniture that his company manufactured. He was discouraged that the Costa Rican government had not offered sufficient support for exporters, especially those that, like his company, needed imported materials for manufacturing.

Productos de Madera, S.A., was one of the largest Costa Rican manufacturers of fine furniture and wood casings for electronic products (e.g., stereos). The company's financial statements are shown in Tables 11–1 and 11–2. During the past five years, Productos de Madera's domestic and export sales had grown substantially, though much of this growth was due simply to inflation. The severe recession of 1982–83 and the continuing Latin American debt crisis had both contributed to the decline in the firm's profits since 1981.

Sr. Michelson was convinced that his prospects for growth in Costa Rica for the next few years were not very good. He expected that he would be able to raise prices to keep up with inflation, but

TABLE 11–1   Productos de Madera Income Statements, 1979–83 *(in millions of colones)*

	1979	1980	1981	1982	1983
Sales					
Local	304	355	388	392	414
Exported	13	26	37	29	33
Production costs					
Labor	90	101	110	123	139
Imported materials	32	39	43	44	47
Local materials	125	148	160	173	186
Administrative costs	11	14	16	17	19
Licensing Fee	6	7	8	8	8
Depreciation	12	12	12	12	12
Interest expense	10	13	15	16	18
Net income before tax	31	47	61	28	18
Tax (40%)					
Net income after tax					

TABLE 11-2 Productos de Madera Balance Sheet, December 31, 1983 *(in millions of colones)*

ASSETS		LIABILITIES	
Cash	25	Accounts payable	61
Marketable securities	5	Notes payable, short-term	28
Accounts receivable	52	Current taxes due	9
Inventories	34	Notes payable, long-term	84
Plant and equipment	137	Net worth (shareholders' equity)	71
Total	253	Total	253

would not be able to substantially increase the amount of furniture sold in Costa Rica. The U.S. market, on the other hand, looked very promising, especially for simple stereo cabinets and possibly for high-quality bookcases and china cabinets, like those produced by Productos de Madera. Dealing only through an agent in Houston, the firm had sold 33 million colones' worth of these products in the United States during 1983. While he was happy with the efforts of his agent, Sr. Michelson wanted to enter the U.S. market directly with his own sales office and perhaps a storage facility (warehouse).

It seemed as though the Costa Rican government was one of the biggest obstacles to his exports. In order to help pay its $10 billion foreign debt, Costa Rica's Central Bank kept all dollar receipts of its exporters, giving them colones in return. Any imported inputs for producing exportable goods required a 115 percent deposit at the Central Bank for about one month before the goods arrived, making the cost rise substantially. By guarding the dollars received and by restricting imports, the government was trying to improve the balance of payments, but it was also squeezing exporters severely.

One positive aspect of government policy was the funding provided by CINDE (the national export-promotion agency) for feasibility studies of export projects. This program offered to lend up to 95 percent of the costs required to carry out such studies, of which half would be given completely free if the export project were undertaken. Using CINDE support, Sr. Michelson had proceeded with a feasibility study to expand his U.S. sales.

As part of the feasibility study, Sr. Michelson had visited Los Angeles, Houston, Atlanta, Miami, and New York during the first four months of 1984 to investigate the possibility of establishing an office. It appeared clear that any of these locations would offer excellent access to the market. He finally chose Miami because of its prox-

TABLE 11–3   Pro Forma Income Statement, Productos de Madera, Inc.   *(in thousands of U.S. dollars)*

	1983	1984	1985	1986	1987	1988
Investment	(900)					
Sales in United States		960	1,133	1,239	1,525	1,810
Costs from San José		636	746	773	1,019	1,187
Cost of insurance and freight		74	85	97	112	129
Administrative costs in Miami		43	52	62	71	86
Financing cost		120	120	120	120	120
Net income before tax						
Tax (40%)						
Net income after tax						

imity to San José, its predominantly Hispanic population, and its importance as the financial capital of Latin America. With the help of a trusted assistant, he drew up a projection of income for the office for the next five years. (See Table 11–3.)

Based on the study's conservative estimates of future costs and revenues from the U.S. project, Sr. Michelson felt justified in going ahead. He was not completely sure of his estimates of costs related to the imports from San José, but he had based them on an estimate of 10 percent devaluation of the colon per year. At the end of 1983 the exchange rate was about 40 colones per dollar.

COMPREHENSION QUESTIONS

Understanding the Main Ideas

Answer the following questions, referring to the case description for information when necessary.

1. What does Sr. Michelson import? What products does his company manufacture?

2. Describe the change that has occurred in the domestic and export sales of Productos de Madera over the past five years. To what can this change be attributed?

3. Compare the outlook for Productos de Madera's growth in the domestic market with its growth potential in the U.S. market.

4. How did Sr. Michelson enter the U.S. market? Was his entry successful?

Photo courtesy of M. Silver Associates, Inc.

5. What capital-budgeting decision must Sr. Michelson make?

6. Why did Sr. Michelson choose Miami as the location for his firm's U.S. office?

Interpreting Financial Reports

The income statement and the balance sheet reflect the financial condition of a company. They are two of the most widely used financial reports. The income statement describes the cash flows of a company over a peiod of time, usually one year. The balance sheet presents the net value of a company's assets, liabilities, and shareholders' equity at the end of a year. The pro forma income statement is used to make projections of future cash flows.

Table 11–1 presents the income statements of Productos de Madera for five years. Table 11–2 consists of the 1983 balance sheet of Productos de Madera. The pro forma income statement in Table 11–3 projects cash flows for the next five years. Study the tables carefully as you consider the following questions.

Table 11–1

Understanding Income Statements

Scan Table 11-1 for the answers to these questions:

1. Which years are covered in the income statements?

2. What does the heading "in millions of colones" refer to?

3. In what country are the local sales made?

4. What was the value of exported sales for the company in 1981?

5. What do the production costs consist of?

6. What items are affected by depreciation?

7. How much did local materials cost the company in 1983?

Interpreting Income Statements

Interpret the meaning of the figures displayed in Table 11–1.

1. Describe the trends in local and exported sales over the past five years.

2. Generally speaking, what happened to the cost of labor, imported materials, and local materials from 1979 to 1983? How can you explain this trend?

3. How did administrative costs change during the five-year period? Give a possible reason for this change.

4. What change took place in interest expense from 1979 to 1983? How can you explain the change?

5. What happened to company profits after 1981?

6. Compute the tax for Productos de Madera for each year from 1979 to 1983, and fill in the blanks in the table. Then calculate the net income after tax and complete that category for each income statement. Are the relationships of net income after tax over the five years different than those of net income before tax?

Table 11–2

Understanding a Balance Sheet

Scan Table 11–2 for the following information.

1. What year is treated in the balance sheet?

2. What are the assets of Productos de Madera?

3. What are the company's liabilities?

4. How much equity do the shareholders have in the company?

5. How much does the company owe in taxes?

6. What is the value of the company's inventories?

Interpreting the Balance Sheet

Now interpret the meaning of the information contained in Table 11–2.

1. Explain the difference between short-term and long-term liabilities.

2. How much debt does the company need to pay off soon?

3. Does the company have enough short-term assets to meet its debt?

4. Is the company in a healthy financial condition?

5. What should the company do to meet its financial obligations?

Table 11–3

Understanding a Pro Forma Income Statement

Answer the following questions while referring to Table 11–3.

1. What does "pro forma" mean?

2. What currency is used in this income statement? In what denomination?

Photo courtesy of M. Silver Associates, Inc.

3. What is the amount of the company's investment in 1983? Why are there parentheses around the figure?

4. How much is the sales projection for 1985?

5. What is the estimated cost of insurance and freight in 1987?

The pro forma income statement will be interpreted in the case analysis.

VOCABULARY DEVELOPMENT

Paraphrasing

Restate the following sentences. Substitute your own words for the underlined expressions.

1. The company had a cash flow problem due to the government policy that required a 115 percent deposit on imported inputs for manufacturing.

2. Sr. Michelson and his assistant made a five-year projection of income for the proposed Miami office.

3. The parent company sold the products at cost to its Miami affiliate.

4. Costa Rica's Central Bank collects the dollar receipts of exporters and exchanges them for colones.

5. The debt crisis in Latin America seriously affected the ability of the countries to borrow money.

6. Exporters felt that the government did not give them enough support.

7. The country's foreign debt exceeded $10 million.

Business Terms

Explain the following terms to a partner. Refer to the case if necessary, but discuss the concepts in your own words.

1. present discounted value

2. capital-budgeting decision

3. cash flow

4. feasibility study

5. debt crisis

CRITICAL THINKING

Think carefully about the following questions. Discuss your ideas with a partner and prepare to present your answers to the class.

1. Why does Sr. Michelson want to enter the U.S. market directly, rather than continuing to sell through his agent in Houston?

2. Since 1981, sales have risen and profits have decreased for Productos de Madera. Explain how this is possible.

3. How is the government of Costa Rica discouraging importers? Give reasons for the government's policies.

4. In what ways is the Costs Rican government encouraging exporters? Why does the government want to help them?

5. What effect will the government's policies have on Costa Rica's balance of payments?

RESEARCH QUESTIONS

Identify a manufacturing firm in your area that exports its products. The firm may be a domestic or a multinational corporation. Interview a company employee who is a native speaker of English to

Photo by Christine U. Grosse

find out the answers to the questions below. Report your findings to the class.

1. What incentives does the government in your country give to exporters?

2. How does the government discourage importers?

3. What capital-budgeting decisions has the company made recently? What criteria does the company use to make the decisions? Which alternatives did the company consider before making its latest decision?

4. Obtain a copy of the company's annual report. Study the income statement and balance sheet in the report, and compare them with those of Productos de Madera in Tables 11–1 and 11–2.

CASE ANALYSIS

Sr. Michelson of Productos de Madera must decide whether to proceed with his plans to establish an office in Miami. Your consulting firm has been hired to help him make this capital-budgeting decision. Reread the case and examine the pro forma income statement in Table 11–3 to help your work group make an analysis of the situation.

Consider the following points before you make your recommendations.

1. The data in the pro forma income statement are based on an estimate of the future exchange rate for colones. What does Sr. Michelson predict will happen to the exchange rate? How accurate do you think his forecast will be?

   What problems might occur if his forecast is inaccurate?

2. Look at the cash flows of the company to judge whether the Miami office is a worthwhile project. That is, consider:

   a. How much money is needed to make the original investment?

   b. What are the future revenues and costs that the project will generate?

3. Calculate the amount of profit that the company will make each year for the next five years. Remember that income is equal to revenue minus costs.

4. How do taxes affect the profitability of the project? Calculate the net income after taxes for each of the five years in the pro forma income statement.

12

THE MORIOKA MANUFACTURING CASE

Japanese management style

Photo by Michal Heron

PREREADING EXERCISE

Discuss the following questions in class before reading the case.

1. In your opinion, what are the reasons for the Japanese "economic miracle" that has occurred since World War II?

2. Many Japanese companies have become extremely successful in international business during the past twenty years. Which Japanese firms and products are well known in your country? In your opinion, why have these Japanese products been so successful?

3. The Japanese style of management has received considerable attention lately because of the success of the Japanese in doing business overseas. What do you know about Japanese management techniques?

4. How would you describe the system of management that is widely used in your country?

THE MORIOKA MANUFACTURING CASE ═══════════

Introduction

During the 1970s and 1980s, worldwide attention has focused on the successes of Japanese firms doing business in the United States, Europe, and elsewhere. Nissan, Toyota, Honda, NEC, Sanyo, Panasonic, and numerous other Japanese brand names have become household words throughout the world. Only two or three decades ago, the largest and most successful international firms came almost exclusively from the United States and Western Europe. How have the Japanese attained such an impressive position in world markets?

As we have already seen in "The U.S. Auto Industry Case," the Japanese auto manufacturers are currently exceeding their American and European competitors in labor productivity and in reducing production costs. In addition, in many industries the quality of Japanese products is perceived to be better than that of firms from other countries. Companies that want to compete successfully against the Japanese will need to achieve similar results in their own business activities. The purpose of this case is to focus attention on the issue of labor productivity, using the Japanese model as a basis for the discussion.

Japanese-style management has been widely analyzed, from its emphasis on long-term employment to its concept of consultative decision making. The central issue in all of the analyses is that Japanese firms appear to pay more attention to *human resources* (i.e., the people who work in the firm) than do firms from other countries. Among the policies used by Japanese firms for human-resource management are these four key elements:

1. long-term employment,
2. slow performance evaluation and promotion,
3. generalist career paths, and
4. consultative decision making.

Since World War II, large industrial corporations in Japan have followed a practice of hiring their employees and managers directly from high school or college, then keeping them employed throughout their careers within the same firm. Very little mobility exists between companies, since Japanese society has come to expect that a person will remain with the same employer until retirement. A very positive aspect of this practice is that it provides job stability for everyone in the firm, so that individuals tend to identify their own interests more with the company, which must perform well if their jobs are to be protected. Also, the company can justify expenditures on the training of employees, knowing that they will remain and offer benefits to the company from their increased skills. The negative aspect (from a Western point of view) is that few socially acceptable choices exist for someone who wishes to change companies during a career, regardless of the reason.

By giving careful evaluation to each employee and manager, Japanese firms demonstrate a sense of caring for the person. Also, by promoting managers through the ranks of management very slowly, the firm conveys to all that long-term performance is what counts. Even after the long initial period, ranks tend to be equal among people with similar seniority, though tasks and compensation become differentiated according to performance. People "save face" by maintaining equal rank with others in their cohort through the years, even while the firm can be managed capably by assigning the key decisions to those who demonstrate the greatest ability to handle them.

A third characteristic of Japanese human-resource management is the use of a generalist career path. That is, Japanese workers and managers are trained in one area of specialization when they join the firm, then rotated among assignments and specializations during their careers so that everyone learns several job skills. Someone hired as a financial analyst may be shifted into the personnel department after four or five years, and then into government-business relations after that. A worker who spends all or most of his time on an assembly line may be moved into repair work and subsequently into another type of assembly-line activity. This policy enhances the flexibility of the firm, because people can be shifted from job to job. It also enables the firm to operate more efficiently by imparting more skills to managers and workers. Thus, no one becomes overspecialized, and everyone spends some time in areas outside of the initial area of specialization, although a worker or manager may return to a preferred specialty after spending time working in other areas.

Finally (in this brief sketch), Japanese firms use a system of consultative decision making, which attempts to pass information about important company activities from the top managers all the way down to the lowest-ranking workers. In particular, decisions that will affect people in any area of the firm are discussed with those people *before* the decision is made, so that the affected workers and managers can voice their opinions and concerns before a problem arises. (For example, an auto company will distribute information about a proposed new assembly line, so that workers affected by the change will be able to see its impact on them and discuss it with their superiors before the change is made.) Because top managers have been rotated through several functional areas of the company, they tend to understand the concerns of people at lower levels and to be responsive to them. Because all employees involved in the decision have the opportunity to raise concerns about potential problems, the firm can avoid errors that otherwise would occur. Ultimately, top management must take responsibility for decisions, so this process does not imply that everyone has equal say in decision making. It is the conscious effort to create communication from bottom to top and top to bottom in the firm, and the fact that this information flow enables managers to make better decisions, that is so crucial here.

Other aspects of Japanese human-resource management could be noted, but those already discussed give a good idea of the basic differences between those firms and their competitors from other countries. One of the major subjects of discussion by managers in the United States during the past few years has been the possibility of transferring some of the Japanese style to U.S. firms. Are people from different countries and cultures similar enough that Japanese practices can be used elsewhere? An illustration of these issues follows.

The Case

The Morioka Manufacturing Company (also known as 2M) is a fairly typical large Japanese corporation that makes abrasives for automobile and industrial clutches, grinding and sanding machines, and specialized polishing equipment. In 1985 the company had about a 70 percent market share in Japan, and had gained almost 25 percent shares in most Western European countries and in North America. Total worldwide sales were over 250 billion yen in 1984.

2M has been evaluating a proposal to acquire a factory formerly operated by Bendix Corporation in California. The factory produced industrial clutches, which Bendix sold to a variety of companies for use in industrial machinery. Because the factory shut down only last year, almost half of the 300 workers formerly employed there would be available to work for 2M. Mr. Yoshi Hajima, the director of 2M's International Division, was wondering about the advisability of investing in the United States at all. He knew that the political pressure on Japan to import more U.S. goods and to invest in the United States to provide more American jobs was strong and most likely would continue through the rest of the decade. 2M could face limitations on its exports to the U.S. market at any time. Since that market now provided about 40 percent of the company's worldwide sales, maintaining U.S. business was critical.

The Bendix factory was not completely outmoded, but it would require substantial investment to upgrade the machinery. The location in California was not a problem for U.S. sales because of the excellent transportation system in the United States. In fact, there was only one negative aspect of the whole idea: Hajima had seen various studies that showed an enormous productivity gap between output per worker in Japan and in the United States. He was not excited about the prospect of dealing with the Americans, even though there was no current threat of a union fight (that is, an effort by workers to organize a union to demand better treatment by management). Other Japanese firms had successfully invested in the U.S. market, though very few of them had achieved anything near the productivity levels of their Japanese operations.

Hajima was most concerned about the need to establish a positive, enjoyable atmosphere in the workplace. He had grown up in such an environment, and he felt complete loyalty to the company that had supported him. He wondered if the U.S. workers, with their average annual turnover rate of almost 10 percent in the chemical industry, could possibly achieve a harmonious relationship with managers and staff that would lead to some degree of company loyalty at 2M in California. He was somewhat encouraged by the telephone conversation he had with a friend at Mitsui's office in San Francisco. The friend had found that the American workers at Mitsui were generally very happy to try many of the Japanese practices, and indeed turnover there was much lower than in comparable U.S. firms. Still, Mr. Hajima was skeptical.

Perhaps the largest difference between the Americans and the Japanese workers with whom Hajima was familiar was the American social preference for rugged individualists versus the Japanese emphasis on commitment to the team (or company) and group achievement. He did not think that the Americans would readily join company-sponsored social groups or do group exercises before work, as in Japan. Though quality circles had shown some promise of acceptance and positive results in American firms, Mr. Hajima did not believe that this was enough to generate the needed level of commitment to the firm. With only a fair understanding of English, he felt quite uncomfortable in trying to assess the situation and reach a decision.

COMPREHENSION QUESTIONS

Discuss the following questions, using your background knowledge and the information you have obtained from reading the case.

1. Explain the Japanese practice of long-term employment. What are the benefits to the company and to the employee?

2. Discuss the process of promotion within a Japanese firm.

3. What is a generalist career path? What are the advantages of this policy?

4. Explain the Japanese system of consultative decision making.

5. What does the 2M Company produce? Describe the market share and total sales of the company for 1984.

6. What proposal is the Morioka Manufacturing Company currently considering? For what reasons is it evaluating the proposal?

VOCABULARY DEVELOPMENT

Understanding Words in Context

Determine the meaning of the underlined words from the context. Explain the business terms to a partner.

1. Japanese employees usually work for the same company for their entire lifetime; they rarely change employers. In contrast, the

Photo by Michal Heron

average annual <u>turnover rate</u> of the U.S. worker was almost 10 percent in the chemical industry.

2. American business managers have shown a preference for <u>rugged individualism</u> instead of team effort as a management style. They believe that their personal qualities and leadership skills are essential to the decision-making process. Although the manager may consult others for advice, she or he is ultimately responsible for taking action. Individual style is very important to the American manager, who assumes individual responsibility for decisions.

3. Japanese firms encourage communication from top to bottom and bottom to top. In this way, managers and employees can exchange ideas about what is right for the company. This <u>information flow</u> helps managers to make better decisions.

4. Although the Bendix factory is thirty years old, its machinery is not completely <u>outmoded</u>. The 2M Company will be able to use the equipment after a substantial investment to modernize it. The firm will need to spend approximately $2 million to <u>upgrade</u> the machinery.

5. For decades Japanese companies have successfully exported products around the world. Honda, Toyota, and Nissan have become <u>household words</u> in many countries. Millions of people are familiar with these Japanese <u>brand names</u>.

Business Terms

Match the business term with its corresponding meaning.

1. long-term employment	a. company employees
2. consultative decision making	b. cost
3. job stability	c. keeping the same job
4. expenditure	d. employment for many years
5. compensation	e. output per worker
6. productivity	f. payment
7. human resources	g. communicative management

Job Descriptions

What are some of the responsibilities of people in the following positions? Give a description of each job.

1. financial analyst
2. personnel manager
3. assembly-line worker
4. government/business-relations specialist
5. production manager
6. treasurer
7. advertising executive
8. general manager
9. trainee

CRITICAL THINKING

Think about the following issues and discuss your ideas with a partner. Be prepared to present your responses to the class.

1. Compare and contrast the management systems in your country and Japan with regard to:

   1. typical length of employment
   2. evaluation and promotion
   3. specialized or generalist career paths
   4. the decision-making process

Photo by Michal Heron

2. Is it possible to transfer a system of management from one country to another? What are some possible obstacles?

3. Discuss the management problems that 2M might encounter if it invests in the Bendix factory in California.

4. Why is the productivity level of Japanese firms located in the United States lower than that of their operations in Japan?

RESEARCH QUESTIONS

The following questions require that you conduct research outside of the classroom.

1. Contact the manager of a Japanese firm in your area (or an American firm if you are in Japan). You may locate the firm through the telephone directory or the local chamber of commerce. Interview him or her about the problems of doing business in another country. Ask for a comparison of common practices in the home country and abroad in these areas:

   1. labor/management relations
   2. concepts of employee loyalty to the firm
   3. turnover rate

4. information flow

5. the decision-making process

6. cultural differences

2. Locate an article in an English-language newspaper or magazine from a library or a newsstand that treats the subject of Japanese management techniques. Read the article for the main idea and supporting details. Prepare a three-to-five-minute oral summary for the class.

3. Several books that describe the system of Japanese management have become international bestsellers. Read *Theory Z* by William Ouchi or *The Art of Japanese Management* by Pascale and Athos. Write a report about what you learn from the book.

CASE ANALYSIS

Mr. Yoshi Hajima, director of 2M's International Division, has asked your group to study the proposal to acquire a factory in the United States. As part of the company's consultative decision-making process, he has requested that you make recommendations concerning two key issues:

1. the desirability of 2M Company's investing in the United States, and

2. the transferability of Japanese management techniques to another country and culture.

Reread the case, then discuss the relevant issues with your group. The following questions can serve as a guide for the case analysis.

1. Evaluate the factory that 2M plans to purchase, as to

   a. location

   b. what it produces

   c. availability of work force

   d. length of time since it was in operation

   e. condition of the machinery

2. Discuss the possibility of limitations on Japanese exports to the United States and the effect of this on the 2M Company.

3. How would the purchase of the factory help to maintain U.S. business for the Morioka Manufacturing Company?

4. How successful were other Japanese firms that invested in the United States?

5. What are the potential problems associated with the purchase? Discuss the following issues and how any difficulties that they present could be resolved.

   a. productivity gap
   b. union fight
   c. investment to upgrade machinery
   d. loyalty to the firm
   e. annual turnover rate
   f. commitment to the team effort

GLOSSARY OF BUSINESS TERMS ═══════════════

account payable a bill that a company must pay by a fixed date.

account receivable a bill due to be paid to a company at a fixed date.

acquisition purchase of controlling ownership of another company.

ad valorem added to the value of a product, such as an *ad valorem* tariff.

adversary opponent, rival firm, competitor.

advertising campaign detailed promotional plan to sell a product or service.

affiliate a company partially or totally owned by another company.

agency a legal form of company allowed to act on behalf of its owner.

assembly line equipment in a factory used to manufacture a final product.

asset balance-sheet item including cash, accounts receivable, inventories, and plant and equipment.

balance of payments account of the flow of transactions between one country and all others during a year.

balance sheet financial statement listing a company's assets, liabilities, and net worth.

bargaining strategy plan for negotiating with a buyer or seller (or with a government).

bidding an offer of a price in a business deal in competition with other firms.

Big Three automakers General Motors, Ford, and Chrysler.

board of directors highest management level of a firm.

bond a form of long-term debt issued by companies to investors.

to boost   to increase.

to borrow   to obtain funds today in promise for repayment in the future.

branch bank   a banking office that is physically located away from the main bank.

brand loyalty   consumer preference to repurchase the product of a particular company.

brand name   a unique name for a product or service associated with one company (e.g., *Chevrolet*, made by General Motors).

bribe   unethical payment, typically to a government representative to obtain a business deal.

business cycle   an upswing followed by a downswing in business conditions that typically occurs every five to seven years.

cable transfer   payment made through instructions wired by telegraph to a bank.

capacity   amount of output of a factory that yields the lowest unit cost of production.

capital-budgeting decision   periodic allocation of financial resources to the major activities of a company.

case study   a detailed description and analysis of a business situation faced by some firm.

cash flow   a receipt or payment of funds made by a company.

C.I.F. (cost of insurance and freight)   an exporting price quotation that includes the seller's price plus the cost of insurance and transportation.

client   customer of a company or bank.

cohort   group of people hired at approximately the same time in a firm.

collateral   asset(s) pledged by a borrower to a lender to guarantee repayment of a loan.

comparative advantage   a production cost difference that favors one country over another.

compensation   payment for services rendered (e.g., wages, salary, fees).

competition   effort of different companies to attract the business of a given company or consumer.

competitive advantage   a strength possessed by a firm that enables it to compete successfully (for example, technology, low costs, or subsidies).

component   a constituent part assembled with other parts into a final product.

computer chips miniature memory and computing components of a computer.

consultant a paid outside adviser to a company.

consultative decision making process of decision making that involves the company's workers (a part of Japanese-style management).

consumer purchaser of a company's products or services.

contract legal agreement, as for the purchase or sale of some item.

cost advantage a competitive advantage held by firms with lower production costs than their rivals.

cost differential difference in production costs between one firm and another or between one location and another.

cost-efficient economical; refers to a process or strategy that minimizes the cost of producing or distributing a product.

creditworthiness a borrower's probable ability to repay funds to be borrowed from a bank, based on the borrower's business condition.

currency cash; means of payment in an economy.

customer client; purchaser of a firm's products or services.

deal business transaction; agreement to buy or sell.

debt obligation to repay money borrowed through such instruments as a bank loan or the issue of bonds.

debt crisis international economic crisis of the 1980s, when most Latin American countries threatened to default on their foreign loans.

decline reduction.

demand amount of a given product or service requested by customers.

deposit money placed in a bank by its clients, in return for interest and other privileges; the basic liability of a bank.

depreciation decrease in the value of equipment over time.

to deregulate to substantially reduce government restrictions on an industry.

devaluation reduction in value of one currency in relation to another currency.

direct investment purchase of ownership and control of a subsidiary in another country.

to disaggregate to divide into component parts.

discount a reduction in price from the original value, often offered in return for early payment.

distributed data processing computing through use of microcomputers in several locations.

distribution channels   method of moving products from the factory to locations where they are sold.

to diversify   (for a company) to enter a new industry or country.

divestiture   disinvestment; partial or total sale of a company's affiliate.

domestic   in the country where the company's headquarters are located.

to dump   to sell in a foreign market at a price below the firm's cost.

Edge Act Corporation   a form of bank in the United States that may legally only carry out international business.

employee   a person who works for a firm, as either a manager or a worker.

employer   a company, bank, government, or other organization that employs workers and managers.

estimate   an attempt to judge the value of some product or service.

eurobond issue   debt instrument (bond) issued by a large company and sold worldwide, by an investment bank with few restrictions.

eurocurrency   a bank deposit denominated in a foreign currency.

eurodollar   a U.S. dollar held as eurocurrency.

exchange rate   the value of one currency in terms of another, typically offered by a commercial bank.

expenditure   use of funds by a firm to purchase goods or services.

to export   to sell to a customer in a foreign country.

feasibility study   an estimate of the future profitability of a possible business activity, such as a factory or office to be built.

financial statement   a presentation of a company's financial performance (e.g., a balance sheet or an income statement).

to fluctuate   (for a financial variable) to move up and down around a trend.

F.O.B. (free on board)   an exporting price quotation that includes the seller's price before shipping costs.

forecast   an estimate of the future value of some key indicator such as sales, interest rates, or wages.

foreign debt   value of loans taken from foreign lenders by all borrowers in a country.

foreign investment   see *direct investment*.

forward contract   a legal agreement dated today for future sale of some financial instrument at a fixed price.

forward rate   exchange rate established today for future sale or purchase of a specific amount of a foreign currency.

free market   a market with few government restrictions on business.

fringe benefits   nonsalary compensation received by employees; for example, paid holidays, medical benefits, and retirement benefits.

funding   source of money to be used in a business activity.

generalist career path   working successively in different company divisions and functions to avoid overspecialization; a process of management development used by Japanese firms.

general manager   chief operating executive of a company's division or affiliate.

GNP (gross national product)   the aggregate value of output of an economy during one year.

to hedge   to protect a company against adverse changes in future business activities.

hike   an increase (e.g., in price).

household word   a well-known company name, brand name, or trademark that consumers recognize.

human resources   the workers and managers in a company, including their skills.

to import   to purchase from a supplier in a foreign country.

import license   legal permit required in some countries to allow purchases from abroad.

incentive   a government policy used to encourage (but not to require) companies to follow the government's chosen goals.

income   money received by an individual for his or her work, or by a company as its profit.

income statement   a financial statement showing a company's revenues, expenses, and profits during the period of one year.

inflation   general increase of prices in a country over time.

input   raw material, part, or assembly used in a business activity.

interest rate   rate of return paid by banks on deposits; the charge made by banks on loans.

internal working capital   cash, accounts receivable and marketable securities used by a firm in its business; short-term assets.

inventory   stock of products held by a firm before sale to customers.

investment   use of funds by a firm to purchase long-term assets or financial instruments.

irrevocable letter of credit   a trade-financing instrument that guarantees payment to the exporter by his bank.

job stability   security of a worker that his or her job will not be terminated.

joint venture   a company affiliate partially owned by another company.

just-in-time-inventory   a strategy used by Japanese companies to minimize a company's inventory by producing in relatively small batches.

to lend   to make funds available to a borrower, with promise of repayment in the future.

letter of credit   a guarantee offered by a bank to assure payment to the seller in an export transaction.

liability   obligations of a firm; specifically, accounts payable, notes payable, long-term debt, and taxes due.

LIBOR (London Interbank Offered Rate)   the base deposit interest rate in the eurocurrency market.

licensing fee   a service charge made by a company for use of its proprietary technology by another company.

linear programming model   mathematical technique used to minimize costs of production and/or transportation.

loan   a legal contract under which a bank makes funds available to a borrower.

loan guarantee   a legally binding agreement made by a bank or government to assure payment to the lender under a loan contract.

logistics   physical distributing of inputs and products in a company.

long-term   any business activity that lasts one year or longer.

majority partner   participant in a joint venture who holds more than 50 percent ownership.

market   economic environment in which buying and selling take place.

market segment   part of the customer market for a given product, as defined by particular characteristics (low cost, high quality, etc.)

market share   percentage of total industry sales made by one company.

to maximize   to achieve the highest possible amount.

mobility   the ability of a worker or a manager to move from one job to another.

to negotiate   to try to reach a business agreement with another firm, person, or government.

net [income]   profit; a firm's revenues minus its costs, after taxes.

outmoded   outdated, obsolete.

output   final product; what a company sells to its customers.

overhead costs   managerial, nonproduction costs of operating a firm.

ownership   possession of the stock (shares) of a firm.

packaging   the container in which a product is sold.

parent company   corporation that owns one or more other corporations.

partner   part owner of a business venture.

payment   delivery of funds for a purchase.

petrochemical   an oil-based chemical product (e.g., plastic, paint).

present discounted value   the estimated value today of a set of future cash flows, as from an investment project.

price quotation   a formal and usually binding statement of a price offered by the seller of a product.

pricing   deciding on the amount to charge for a product.

prime rate   interest rate charged by major U.S. commercial banks to their most creditworthy borrowers.

product   basic output that a firm sells to customers.

productivity   output per man-hour; output generated by a production factor during a given time period.

profit   net income after tax.

profitability   return on assets, on equity, or on sales; the key measure of a firm's performance.

profit remittance   transfer of profits from an affiliate company to the parent company.

pro forma [income statement]   estimated financial statement for a future business activity.

projection   estimate of a future value.

promotional strategy   plan of action for advertising a product to the public.

proposal   offer of a business agreement by one firm seeking a contract with another.

to purchase   to buy a product or service.

quality circle   a team of workers and managers who work together to try to improve the quality of the firm's product.

raw materials   basic production inputs, such as oil, copper, coal.

raw production data   records of a factory's output, before they have been analyzed by the firm's managers.

receipt   a legal document proving purchase of a product or service.

recession   a persistent downturn in economic conditions in a country, typically lasting for two to four years.

to regulate   (for a government) to place limitations on the functioning of a market or an industry.

remote terminal   a television screen in one location connected to a computer's central processing unit in another location.

representative office   a banking office that may not provide services directly but may refer clients to other offices of the same bank.

restriction   a limitation placed on business activity, typically by a government.

retirement   period in a person's life after ending his or her career.

return (on investment)   net income after tax divided by amount of money invested; a basic measure of profitability.

revenue   money received for sales.

risk   possibility of loss, typically measured by estimate of possible future outcomes.

risk avoidance   a business strategy of pursuing low risk ventures and demanding a high return for risky ventures.

rival firm   competitor.

rugged individualism   a preference for nonconformity and personal self-realization (a stereotype often attributed to U.S. managers and workers).

sales   the value of goods sold; revenue.

securities   stocks, bonds, and other financial instruments that pledge fulfillment of an obligation.

shareholders' equity   stock; value of a firm to its owners.

shipment   physical movement of goods from one location to another, or the goods that are being moved.

shop floor   the inside of a factory, where manufacturing is done.

spot exchange rate   price of one currency in terms of another for a transaction today.

spread   the margin a bank charges for profit above its cost of funds.

stock   a share of ownership in a corporation.

strategy   plan of action used by a firm to achieve its goals.

subsidiary   one company that is owned by another company.

subsidy   financial support offered by a government to help a company.

supply   amount of a product or service offered by its producer.

syndicated eurocurrency loan loan made by a group of European banks at an interest rate lower than the domestic one.

target country host country; nation chosen by a firm for its sales.

tariff tax charged by a government on imports.

tax holiday a form of subsidy that allows a firm to pay no tax for a specified time period.

top end the most expensive, usually highest-quality, segment of a market.

top management the highest-level operating managers of a company.

trade commerce; exports and imports.

transaction purchase or sale agreement; a business "deal."

Treasury bill a short-term borrowing instrument issued by the U.S. Treasury.

trend tendency; direction (up or down) of business activity.

tubing pipe often used in plumbing.

turnover rate at which people leave a company.

to undercut to establish a price below that of competitors.

union labor organization established by workers to bargain with companies.

unit cost total cost divided by number of items.

up-front fee service charge made by banks at the time of a loan for borrowing.

to upgrade to improve a plant and equipment; to modernize.

upswing (sales) an increase in volume sold; (business cycle) upward movement of national income in the cycle.

U.S. domestic bank loan loan from a U.S. bank within the U.S. market.

U.S. domestic bond issue long-term debt instrument issued by a large company and sold by an investment bank in the U.S. market

U.S. domestic equity issue issue of stock by a company in the U.S. market.

vertical integration expansion by a firm to include production of the components of its product, or to include production of the product of which the firm produces a component.

wages compensation paid to workers.

warehouse storage facility, typically for manufactured goods.

INDEX